About the Author

Kathryn Lee holds a Bachelor of Science degree from Skidmore College. She is a former model, business executive, member of assorted boards and volunteer organizations and past veterinary technician. A lifelong dog owner/lover of Dachshunds, Poodles, Cocker Spaniels, Cockapoos and beloved Golden Retrievers, she has bred Golden Retrievers since 1990 and Goldendoodles since 2002.

Honey May Lee

Dedication

Dedicated to Honey May Lee, 1994-2005, and Chewey Scott, 1997-2005, my beloved Golden Retrievers.

Chewey Scott

About Our Cover Dog

Meet Ginger, a one-year-old Goldendoodle bred by the author, Kathryn Lee. Ginger's family describes her as sweet, gentle and athletic. This sporty girl loves to chase tennis balls, but she always finds time to relax with her owners and a tasty peanut butter biscuit.

Goldendoodle

By Kathryn Lee

Welcome to the world of this charming Doodle who is worth his weight in gold.

Acknowledgments

The publisher wishes to thank the following Goldendoodle owners and breeders for cooperating with photographer Mary Bloom and/or sending photographs of their dogs for use in this book: Frank Anderson, Maddy Bailey, Heather Bernatchez, Mary Lee Blackwell, Blazing Star kennels, Amy Cabre, the Cornell family, Reed Donahue, Noreen Fisher, Audrey Garden, Katrina Grady, Holly Haringa, Sharon Janikies, the Kehoe family, Tracy King, Polly Kurasch, Amy Lane (Fox Creek kennels), Deirdre Lightsey, N. Beth and Jeffrey S. Line (IDOG), the Marble family, Monica (Joy) Parkin (ShadyMaple Doodles), Russ Polen, Diane Richards, Cindy Stephens, Laurie Warren, Kathryn Yamartino and last but not least, our author, Kathryn Lee.

Kennel Club Books®, the country's only major publisher of exclusively dog books, proudly presents its *Designer Dog Series*™ to celebrate the Goldendoodle's coming-out party. Continuing in its bold effort to produce a unique line of dog books, Kennel Club Books® releases the first ever books on the specific designer-dog crossbreeds. The company has also released many *Special Limited Editions* and *Special Rare-Breed Editions* on various unusual breeds.

Visit the publisher's website at www.kennelclubbooks.com to read more about the unique library of books available to dog lovers around the world.

KENNEL CLUB BOOKS®
Designer Dog
SERIES™

GOLDENDOODLE
ISBN: 1-59378-671-9

Copyright © 2006, 2007
Kennel Club Books® a division of BowTie, Inc.
40 Broad Street, Freehold, NJ 07728 USA
Printed in South Korea

Photography by:
Mary Bloom

with additional photos by
Mary Lee Blackwell and
Isabelle Français.

10 9 8 7 6 5 4 3 2

Contents

Introducing the

Goldendoodle

Sue Hazard of New England recalls an unexpected pregnancy of a neighbor's brown Poodle by a Golden Retriever in the fall of 1963.

Wishing to assist her friend with this surprise occurrence, she began planning to take in one of the puppies as a pet. Excitedly, at Christmas that same year, her family became the proud owners of one of the first known "Goodles" ever in the New England area. The dogs were called "Goodles" at the time, she says, "Because we did not know what else to call them."

"On Christmas Eve, my husband told our two daughters that he was going out to get a turkey, and he came home with this adorable puppy under his coat. She immediately hid under a chair for the rest of the night, and my parents, who were visiting, were convinced she might just stay there forever, but she did not. We named her Holly, and she went everywhere with us. She had a fluffy blonde curly coat and was a wonderful puppy with absolutely no bad habits. These were the days before obedience schools, dog trainers, leash laws and crates."

In time Holly was joined by two more human sisters and more pets too—a cat, a Golden Retriever named Daffy who had been cast off from a breeder because of an eye condition called entropion and another "mistake" Goodle named Winnie, who also had many fine attributes. Holly remained so endearing to all.

"On long ski trips north she would sleep contently, curled up at my feet, so happy to be along with the family. She was also so smart and easily trained. She would sit, lie down and give you her paw, but her favorite trick was being able to add and subtract, and even multiply. She would bark the answer and when you slightly touched the top of her head, she would stop. It was quite a trick!

"Everyone in the neighborhood and friends wanted a 'Holly.' I was able to find a rare ad for a Golden mother and a black Poodle father combo, and so some of my friends were able to get their Goodles also."

One of those friends is Mercy Wheeler, who recalls equally as well the day she got her black Goodle puppy, Baba, for ten dollars. She tells of living in Needham, Massachusetts in the mid-1970s, and one particular day on which she eagerly waited to finish up her weekly tennis match with her good friend, Sue. This was the day that she was going to pick up her new Goodle puppy! She recalls how adorable all of these curly black puppies were, the likes of which she had never seen before. She and her family adored Baba; she was a wonderful pet. Since Mercy was a tennis coach for the high school, Baba became the team mascot and was adored by all. She appeared in team pictures, always with a beloved tennis ball in her mouth.

The years went by and they were kind years of great joy and love, but in time

This adorable designer Doodle is bursting onto the scene.

Holly, Winnie and Baba passed on, leaving their families with wonderful memories. Their owners looked and looked for more Goodles, but were never able to find any of these incredibly affectionate, intelligent, unique, loved and wanted-by-all canine beings. What they did not know was that they and their wonderful "mistake" Goodles were on the cutting edge of a rising tide of new thought and technology in the breeding, selection, care and

The Goldendoodle promises to add fun and love to your life...he'll even shake on it.

training challenges associated with them. Also, they are shocked by the scarcity of quality Goldendoodles, requiring the smart and informed owner to plan ahead.

training of dogs throughout the United States and abroad.

Remember again, Sue described her Goodle puppy as a fluffy, blonde, curly, wonderful puppy with "absolutely no bad habits." Yet, "These were the days before obedience schools, dog trainers, leash laws and crates." Now, these are the days of leash laws, the Internet, advanced communications, new breeding technologies, new veterinary disciplines and many new training resources. There are excellent advantages to all of these new advancements, but there are also pitfalls along the way. I know that both Sue and Mercy were overwhelmed by not only the cost of today's Goodles, now known as Goldendoodles, but also by all of the new marketing and

Mercy now lives happily with a beloved Goldendoodle named Sweep, who was acquired during the Boston Red Sox's World Series victory in 2004. She calls Sweep the most wonderful and beautiful dog she has ever had, thanks to the great efforts and skill of good breeders who produce the best Goldendoodles possible, as opposed to the "mistake" Goodles of the past. Mercy also proudly reports that Sweep is an icon at a Cape Cod dog park, where he always draws a crowd of admirers, as all Goldendoodle owners will tell you of their dogs. Mercy adds, "Sweep is easy to maintain, loves other dogs and rolls over for tummy rubs in an instant!"

Sue Hazard, who found the original Goodles for her friends in the 1970s, is delighted to soon present one of her daughters and several grandchildren with a female Goldendoodle puppy. Admittedly, it has been a bit of a culture shock for Sue, watching the Goodles of the past become today's "designer" Goldendoodles that have been written about in major publications and have made appearances on national television networks. There are and continue to be literally hundreds of articles in local, national and international periodicals commenting on the phenomenon of the Goldendoodle.

Thus it is the intent of this book to offer the history of the modern-day Goldendoodle and provide helpful hints and guidelines that will enable those like Sue and Mercy to continue finding new Goldendoodles for their grandchildren, assist people who are looking to add one of these wonderful new pets to their lives or just educate those who wish to learn more about the Goldendoodle, a dog that has leapt into the public's consciousness.

The reader should feel secure with any sites or sources referenced herein. Further, if finding information elsewhere on Goldendoodles, the reader should return to this book and the sources referenced to check on the alternative source's credentials. It is also important to recognize the remarkable behind-the-scenes efforts that are making the Goldendoodle a rising star, destined to be a favorite in homes across North America and around the world.

And so off we go! It is time for the Goldendoodle to take center stage!

The Goldendoodle is just plain fun to be around.

Combine the Poodle and Golden Retriever

The Modern Origins of the
Goldendoodle

T he history of the Golden-
doodle begins with a salute to Australian breeders and
their creation of the Labradoodle. They saw early on a
need for a dog that would cause few problems for
allergy-prone people who were in need of an assistance dog. Wally
Conran of Royal Guide Dogs in Australia sought to pair and refine
the excellent proven guide-dog abilities of the Labrador Retriever
with the hypoallergenic qualities of the Standard Poodle. The
results were wonderful.

Thereafter, Dr. Kate Schoeffel, a geneticist and veterinarian in
Condobolin, New South Wales, began breeding male Miniature
Poodles with female Labrador Retrievers to yield Labradoodles
for family pets. With credit to these two pioneering professionals
and the Labradoodle breeding and research centers that were
established in Australia, the Labradoodle has become an
outstanding service dog as well as a highly sought-after family pet
worldwide. This leads us back to the birth of the Goldendoodle in
the United States, Canada and other countries.

It seems perfectly logical to open-minded breeders, ever
seeking to improve on a variation on a theme, when seeing and
reading about the success of the Labradoodle, to want to meld the
wonderful qualities of the Golden Retriever with the fine skills and

for one fabulous hybrid: the Goldendoodle!

Smart, people-loving and very sociable, Goldendoodles offer the best of all possible worlds.

to watch a dog, sitting in his yard on a bright morning and lifting his head high to sniff the miraculous scents that he detects on a gentle breeze, to note this canine phenomenon. Further, did you ever notice how a dog's nose, along with his keen sense of hearing, enables him to tell that someone has arrived home long before a human family member even realizes that a person is at the door?

Poodles and Goldens (like all dogs) are omnivorous, meaning that they like to eat both meat and vegetables. Both breeds also have strong hunting, retrieving and water-loving backgrounds. (It is generally thought that the Poodle is a direct descendant of the 16th-century Water Dog of England, which was popular with hunters, and/or the Irish Water Spaniel, an adept retriever with a curly coat.)

The Poodle is also known for its wonderful hypoaller-genic coat and is regarded as one of the smartest breeds in the world. It is an active, sociable dog that loves human companionship.

The Golden Retriever, English in origin, descends

qualities of the Poodle as well. Let's discuss some of the remarkable traits of the Golden Retriever and the Poodle.

Both Golden Retrievers and Poodles, being canines, have excellent hearing, some four times better than that of humans, especially when it comes to higher-pitched sounds. Both breeds have keen senses of smell, with their noses being their greatest sensory organs. You need only from dogs known as "Wavy-Coated Retrievers" and the Tweed Water Spaniel, eventually resulting in the beloved Golden Retriever. Golden Retrievers are very people-oriented, gentle, loving and calm, and are exceptionally suited for guide dog and therapy work. Like the Poodle, the Golden Retriever is very smart and easily trained, and loves water, retrieving and hunting. The breed does shed heavily and does not have hypoallergenic qualities, which is a problem for those suffering from allergies.

Through the years, Golden Retrievers began being bred to meet certain breed standards as well as the demands of the breed's popularity, which ultimately gave rise to various genetic concerns. This resulted in careless inbreeding and overbreeding by some irresponsible "breeders," thus leading to the existence of serious health issues within the breed's gene pool. Nonetheless, there are many dedicated Golden breeders who are very selective and work to eradicate these genetic problems through careful breeding.

Now that we know more about the two outstanding pure-bred parent breeds, let us learn more about how our Golden Retriever/Poodle mixes, the "Goodles" of the 1970s, eventually became known as the Goldendoodle. Amy Lane, formerly of Maryland and now of Fox Creek kennels in West Virginia, was a longtime breeder of Golden Retrievers. Intrigued by the success of the Labradoodle, she bred her first litter of Goldendoodles shortly after meeting a Labradoodle. The puppies' beautiful fluffy

A cousin of sorts, the Labradoodle derives from crosses of the Labrador Retriever and the Poodle.

A dream of a Doodle: can anyone deny the Goldendoodle's charm, talent or cuteness?

dog as their Australian forebears.

This success led Amy to find another avenue in which Goldendoodles could excel in service work. In 2005 she donated a first-generational cross of a pure-bred Golden Retriever and a pure-bred Standard Poodle, known in the world of Doodles as an "F_1" puppy, named "Sparky" to the St. Francis of Assisi Service Dog Foundation in Roanoke, Virginia. This service organization has a prison inmate program where Sparky rotates in and out of the prison to ensure a well-rounded dog for service work. All reports convince Amy that Sparky will be a wonderful helper to someone who needs him. The program director who trains him cites Sparky as "one of the best-bred dogs we've ever received."

After several years of producing F_1 (Golden to Poodle cross) standard Goldendoodles, Amy decided to try "downsizing" for owners interested in Goldendoodles but needing smaller dogs. She used a Miniature Poodle, "Tarzan," to produce her first miniature Goldendoodle litter

light coats inspired her to call them "Goldendoodles." Further, knowing that the Poodle has long been recognized as one of the smartest breeds of dog, she felt that her Goldendoodles should be every bit as capable of service-dog work as the Labradoodles had proven to be for their Australian developers.

As of May 1, 2005, one of Lane's own Goldendoodles, named "Richter," whom she donated to Guide Dogs of America in Los Angeles for training as a guide dog for the blind, went on to become a graduate guide dog. Another of her Goldendoodles, "Neka," will soon follow, proving that indeed Goldendoodles are every bit the dream Doodle via artificial insemination with a vet's help. She had previously decided it would be important to keep a few pups to raise, and then determine whether the miniatures had the same wonderful attributes as the standards: sound minds and bodies, excellent health and coats that shed minimally or not at all. The two females Amy kept had good bites, strong Golden Retriever traits and more relaxed coats. At one year of age Amy determined that the F_1 miniature Goldendoodle was the most well-rounded family pet she had ever known. This versatile mid-size dog began appearing in TV commercials, excelling as a therapy dog and being used as the featured model in dog-training DVDs and books.

Amy Lane is generally credited with giving our modern-day Goldendoodle its now universally accepted and delightful name. However, it is more fun to hear some of this interesting story in Amy's own words: "I named the breed 'Goldendoodle' and caught quite a bit of flack from Beverley Manners, one of the original breeders of Australian Labradoodles. The name

Goldendoodle just seemed to fit. I was accused of trying to capitalize on the popularity of the Labradoodle. I was given other options of names to use, such as PoodleReivers, Goldiepoos or Groodles, but the name Goldendoodle stuck.

"I do know that I was one of the first to be breeding for F_1 standard Goldendoodles, but I don't believe I produced the very first litter. I was breeding AKC Golden Retrievers and was helping another breeder with the marketing and placing of her Labradoodles. I had a stray pony come to my farm, and he kicked and killed my wonderful Golden stud. I knew I had to replace him...it was a long, hard decision. I decided then, instead, to purchase my first Poodle stud—families fell in love with the Goldendoodle pups. The rest is history!"

Indeed it is history in the making—past, present, and future—with more stories to come about the remarkable efforts to develop Golden-doodles as a breed with the potential to be one of the most popular family pets and very worthy service/therapy dogs in America, Canada and abroad.

Author Kathryn Lee with two of her foundation dams:

The Development of the
Goldendoodle

The Goldendoodle phenomenon

that started in the United States has also found its way to our friends in Canada. Many excellent breeders of Goldendoodles and the Goldendoodle breeder/owner central database, which we will discuss further, are, in fact, of Canadian origin and residence. In fact, many of the Goldendoodle puppies and adult dogs you may see with their owners on the streets and in parks in the US have Canadian backgrounds.

Such an exemplary fine breeder working hard to develop, advance and protect the evolution of the Goldendoodle hails from British Columbia. Monica (Joy) Parkin of ShadyMaple Doodles (www.shadymapledoodles.com) shares her interesting journey from pure-bred breeder to Goldendoodle breeder. Perhaps at this juncture it is important to comment that quality Goldendoodle breeders around the world are every bit as reliable and responsible as pure-bred breeders claim themselves to be. Sometimes there is a prejudice toward the Goldendoodle (and other similar hybrids) by pure-bred breeders, who may sometimes speak with disrespect toward Goldendoodle breeders, which is decidedly undeserved, as we will see from Monica (Joy) Parkin's story and more to follow. As for those who still seek to discredit the Goldendoodle and their reputable developers/breeders, it is important to remind them that many beautiful roses in the world

Dandy Doodle, the Poodle, and Lady Star, the Golden Retriever.

IMPORTANCE OF HEALTH CLEARANCES

Regardless if you are buying a dog of pure-bred or mixed-breed heritage, it is important to see the parents' health clearances. Parents with good hearts, eyes clear of cataracts and well-structured hips will help the pup's buyer feel better about the overall health of the puppy he intends to purchase.

Be certain to see both parents' hip certifications from the Orthopedic Foundation for Animals (OFA) or PennHIP, and current eye clearances from the Canine Eye Registration Foundation (CERF). The hips should be tested as Fair, Good or Excellent. The eyes must be cataract-free and free from other canine genetic eye problems, and the heart strong and healthy. Never purchase a puppy from a breeder without having seen the parents' clearances!

today would not exist if their originators had listened to nay-sayers. So now, on to Monica (Joy) Parkin's discovery of the Goldendoodle in British Columbia:

"I had bred and shown pure-bred dogs since I had my first litter of Corgi pups as a Junior Handler back in 1987. In the years that followed I continued to own, train and show two shedding breeds: Pembroke Welsh Corgis and German Shepherds. I put obedience titles on a number of dogs and championships on others.

"My first Corgi was sired by a famous stud dog owned by an all-breed judge, and though he received his championship and obedience title on the same day, he was diagnosed shortly afterwards with juvenile cataracts and von Willebrand's disease. I was heartbroken that my first breeding dog would have to be neutered but was more dismayed when I was told by

the breeder-judge who owned
the sire that I should breed the
dog anyway as he had great
'type.' I continued with pure-
bred dogs but searched for a
better, healthier line of dogs. I
eventually settled on German
Shepherds, not the show
variety but the German
working variety.

"I loved the way the
Germans run their breeding
programs, as they require dogs
to pass both a hip x-ray and a
rigorous working test before
they can be certified to be
bred. I wanted to breed dogs
like that, dogs that not only
looked good but were genetically sound with stable,
trainable temperaments. The
only problem was that as
much as I loved German
Shepherds, I didn't love the
shedding and I didn't like the
prey drive that was part of
their working heritage. I
wanted a dog whose purpose
for being bred wasn't to win in
the show ring or to sniff out
criminals but just to be a

Healthy, happy and ready to
"go fish"...

wonderful family pet, a dog that was neither aggressive nor timid and that could lie on the couch beside me without leaving buckets of hair behind.

"After much research I settled on a Standard Poodle and finished his championship. Despite the fact that he was a stunning-looking dog, and though I loved his smarts and lack of shedding hair, I quickly decided that this was not the breed for me. It was clear that this Standard Poodle was too high-energy and required too much grooming for the average pet owner. He could open doors, could jump a 7-foot-high fence and experienced severe separation anxiety every time we left the house without him. As an experienced dog owner, I was barely able to manage him and couldn't visualize ever placing a Poodle pup like him with a first-time pet owner and expecting the person to be successful at raising and training the dog without a lot of professional help.

"Not all Standard Poodles are like this, and they can still be a wonderful choice for people with severe allergies, but I didn't have severe allergies and I didn't have the heart to try again with a new Poodle from different bloodlines. By this point I was at a loss as to what kind of dog would possibly meet all of my requirements when I stumbled across Doodles on the Internet and felt like I had found what I had been searching for the last 15 years. As a child I had a Poodle mix and, looking back, he was the best dog I had ever owned. He was a Benji-type dog who had a low-maintenance, non-shedding coat, was great with us kids and was a healthy dog who lived for 15 years, from when I began school in grade one until I was in university.

"Despite my great experience with my own SPCA (Society for the Prevention of Cruelty to Animals) Doodle, Sandy, as a child, I had been a Canadian Kennel Club member for so many years and thought that the only good dog was a pure-bred dog.

"Therefore it was with great reluctance and trepidation that I bred our first litter of Goldendoodles in late 2002.

I was worried they might take on the temperament of a highly independent Standard Poodle rather than that of a laid-back, owner-devoted Golden. I was skeptical until the pups arrived and exceeded my every expectation.

"They were calm pups with gentle, loving personalities, and I have never felt as personally satisfied as a breeder as I do looking at a new batch of Goldendoodle puppies. To date, they have all had the non-aggressive, non-independent temperaments I was striving for, and as a bonus they each have their own unique look and character. The possibilities of coat, size and color constantly challenge my knowledge of genetics, and the owners never cease to impress me with the thoroughness of their research and their commitment to being responsible pet owners. When we first started out, the vast majority of our sales were [to the US], but as our program grows we are finding that more and more of our customers are local.

"In 2003, with the assistance of Kathy Burgess at DoodleQuest in Kentucky and our wonderful veterinarian Dr. Bruce Renooy at Van Isle Veterinary in British Columbia, we also started a mini Goldendoodle program that was the first of its kind in Canada. We are now teaching other breeders to do artificial insemination using advanced reproduction techniques such as multiple sires with DNA parentage testing, surgical insemination and overnight shipping.

"Since that first litter of minis we have learned enough about advanced canine reproduction techniques to be able to expand our gene pool and choice of studs. Our mini stud dog, 'Coco,' whose genes would once have been limited to siring dogs within reasonable travel distance, has now sired litters as far away from us as Kentucky and Boston.

"We continue to advance our knowledge of artificial insemination and have found that Doodle breeders are in a class of their own when it comes to their knowledge of genetic testing and advanced reproduction techniques. The Doodle breeders we have met and befriended along the way are highly educated dog breeders who are devoted to producing healthy dogs from tested parents. The ones we know can tell you in detail the difference between the different hip testing methods and are working hard to create healthy, happy family pets and service dogs. We continue to be amazed and thrilled by the amount of knowledge and support that exists in the Goldendoodle community and is freely shared by all who are willing to listen and to breed responsibly."

Of note in Monica (Joy) Parkin's story is her reference to working with other breeders internationally, such as Kathy Burgess of DoodleQuest near Lexington, Kentucky. Kathy is a former Golden Retriever breeder and bred the world's first Goldendoodle litter that used a Toy Poodle as a stud via artificial insemination. She has been thrilled with the "health, temperament and structure" of her pups thus far. She hopes to continue experimental breedings for special colors and coat types and cites that DoodleQuest now has pups in the US, Canada and overseas.

"DoodleQuest has donated many pups as assistance dogs for the disabled and has also donated to specialty organizations. It is nice to see so many special-needs individuals, many with allergies, to finally have their own special dogs. Assistance dogs open the world up for their disabled owners and help them cross social barriers," writes Kathy.

Having shared with you these particularly enlightening stories of pioneers in the Goldendoodle, it is also of import to include the following words from Jackie Clark of the Pacific Assistance Dogs (PADS) hearing-dog program. PADS is an excellent program to which this writer can attest firsthand, having had an elderly parent with hearing loss who was dependent on her pet dog for hearing concerns. Jackie Clark says the following:

"Pacific Assistance Dogs was first introduced to the miniature Goldendoodle in the fall of 2003 when Kathy Burgess of DoodleQuest donated two unrelated male puppies to their hearing-dog program. 'Dash' did not qualify for the program due to a lack of interest in responding to sounds, but has been adopted as a companion

Meet one of the friendliest
Goldendoodles on the block:
could therapy-dog "Buddy"
have a better name? His pal
JoAn Luther doesn't think so!

by a woman with hearing loss who was looking for a well-trained pet. 'Chase' excelled at his sound work and has recently been placed with a deaf woman with several young children. Chase alerts her to sounds within the home such as the baby crying, the doorbell, the telephone ringing, the alarm clock in the morning and, very importantly, the smoke alarm, should it go off.

"Deafness is an invisible disability; people do not know you are deaf by looking at you. It is often mistaken for rudeness or a lack of mental acuity on the part of the deaf person. Having a hearing dog like Chase accompany you in public makes the public take note of your disability so that they can be sure to face you directly when speaking and speak slowly. Chase's partner has also been trained to watch his body language; he is very in tune to the noises around him and will respond to screeching tires, approaching

On the wings of love, here's Angel, donated to PADS from ShadyMaple Doodles.

sirens and other important sounds.

"PADS's most recent acquisition is a black-and-white miniature Goldendoodle puppy donated by Shady-Maple Doodles. Even as a very young pup of 14 weeks old, 'Angel' is very tuned in to the world around her. The highlight of her day is getting to work on her sounds—so far she has mastered responding to a beeping timer and the ringing telephone, and she is currently working on the smoke alarm. When Angel hears one of her sounds, she has been trained to run over to her trainers, jump up onto their legs to get their attention (barking for attention doesn't work when you're deaf!) and lead them back to the sound, where there just happens to be a yummy jackpot of treats for her efforts.

"Over the years, PADS has found that Miniature Poodles and Poodle crosses are the ideal dogs for the deaf and hard-of-hearing. These dogs tend to have the energy level required to always be on the ready if a sound should go off, are confident in public

situations and bond well to their partners."

Interestingly to note, as of 2005 seven trials of the PADS program using standard Labradoodles were not successful. Could it be that Goldendoodles are turning out to be a bit superior to this other Doodle breed in some areas?

It is important to comment that in the world of Golden-doodles, there are those who adore standards and those who admire miniatures. Both are wonderful, and it is merely a matter of a family's prefer-ence in choosing. Let's hear from one of the early standard Goldendoodle breeders. An excellent Canadian breeder, Nikki of Blazing Star kennels is firmly committed to the development of her fine line of standard Goldendoodles and concentrates on bringing exceptional colors into her lines. Her story is also an interesting one that outlines many sacrifices that good breeders make to bring the highest quality to the better-ment of the Goldendoodle. Far too few breeders can make the similar claim of producing only the finest offspring

Help is on the way...the Goldendoodle takes to therapy work quite naturally. This miniature Doodle is Jake.

border directly above the Minnesota/North Dakota boundary. We started out a number of years ago with the acquisition of our first pure-bred Labrador Retriever.

"In the fall of 2000 we had to sell our farmland and adjacent yard and dwelling due to poor farming conditions. We moved just a few miles away and purchased a 10.2-acre yard with out-buildings that we planned on converting into kennels to expand our program. As I searched the Internet for various breeds to consider, I happened upon the Labra-doodle, did some research and became very interested in this crossbreed due to its genetic diversity, which lessens the chances of health problems.

"Producing happy, healthy puppies with sound family-based temperaments has always been our top priority. In my research on Labradoodles, I was introduced to Golden-doodles and was immediately hooked. When starting out, of

possible. Here is Nikki's story:

"We are a family-owned and -run breeding facility that specializes in Goldendoodles, Labradoodles and Aussie-doodles. We are located in southern Manitoba, just a short distance from the United States course, it took a few years to build our base of breeding stock, but by 2002 we were on our way with our Doodles.

"We are very proud to produce a variety of colors, both F_1 (first-generation cross) and F_{1B} (backcross) standard Goldendoodles weighing 60–80 pounds. The colors we have produced to date are very light cream, cream, gold, apricot, red, black, blue and the prized rare chocolate. We are now frequently asked for breeding stock by other breeders for their programs, so our program stretches now to various parts of the United States through other breeders.

"I've found that families purchasing Goldendoodles are looking for a friendly family pet that is hypoallergenic and light- to non-shedding, and this is exactly what they get. A bright spot in our program is our donation program, where we donate a puppy to children needing a companion or a service dog. It is such a joy to provide this service to families in need. We have Doodles doing service work with children who have cerebral palsy, autism and heart conditions. We also have Doodles graduating to become

Cuddle up with a bundle of Doodle love.

licensed therapy dogs for hospitals and retirement/ nursing homes, not to mention grief counseling. I think this part of our program brings me the most pride.

"As with anything else there are downfalls; for us it has been

Snowy nose, warm heart!

finding good-quality breeding stock in the Golden Retrievers. Hip dysplasia is a very big problem with Golden Retrievers, [which] we learned the hard way with three of our breeding females' testing positive for hip dysplasia. We test all of our dogs prior to breeding; ensuring that they are of sound health and hips are main concerns. Raising these dogs from pups to over a year old and then finding them to be dysplastic and having to rehome them set our program back a number of years in the beginning. It was very difficult to accept, literally heartbreaking, but it was an important part of our learning process.

"In conclusion, we have truly enjoyed our decision to add these amazing Doodle breeds to our program. They are incredibly amazing dogs, forever loving of people and other dogs, gentle and sweet, silly and goofy, all at the same time. They have done so well in family situations with children of all ages and have made wonderful companions to the elderly."

The author thanks Nikki for her thoughtful story and thanks all of the others, herein mentioned, for sharing about the behind-the-scenes development of Goldendoodles. There are many more fine breeders working hard to keep the Goldendoodle the highest quality family pet in which someone can invest for his family and future. Yet, before we discuss how to find your quality Goldendoodle, we must first discuss an important secret about our Goldendoodles—read on!

So you think I'm
gorgeous...just turn the page
and see how alluring we
Goldendoodles really are!

One part Poodle and one part Golden

The Allure of the
Goldendoodle

We have marveled at the intricacies of the Goldendoodle's development throughout the world, with Miniature and Toy Poodles now being used as stud dogs by means of artificial insemination. The sharing of knowledge between breeders from different parts of the country has produced diverse gene pools and a bright future on the Goldendoodle's horizon. Such innovative breeding techniques are producing not only size variations in Goldendoodle puppies but also color variations ranging from the traditional very light whites and creams to blacks, silvers and grays; browns or chocolates; light and dark apricots and parti- or multi-colored Doodles.

We have heard breeders talk of the exceptional temperaments, intelligence and looks, as well as the low-shedding and low-allergenic properties, of these beautiful canine beings known as Goldendoodles. Yet, what is the true allure of these often-dubbed "designer dogs" of today? The answer is a wonderful and much-needed concept to be re-introduced into the breeding world. That concept is a phenomenon known as "hybrid vigor," and breeders often refer to their Goldendoodles as "hybrids." Simply put, hybrid vigor (technically "heterosis") refers to the tendency of the first cross ("first filial" or "F_1") of two parent strains to grow better, stronger, healthier, more

yields a sextet of vigorous, adorable hybrids.

fertile and more intelligent than either parent breed. In the animal world, the more generations that the parents have been kept apart, the better. Thus, the first-cross hybrid offspring tend to have fewer genetic maladies in common within their gene pools since the parent breeds are unrelated. This is indeed a positive thing. Let's now compare this type of breeding to the pure-bred gene pools that have been circulating for centuries in many cases, with the same going around over and over again—nothing new, and nothing new even wanted!

Good breeders of pure-bred dogs have watched helplessly as their champion stud dogs, on which they spent large sums of money, breed litters with repeated genetic faults. Owners of pure-bred Golden Retrievers, for example, may see their dogs dying younger and younger from increased susceptibilities to various diseases or disorders that keep showing up in the breed no matter what is done to prevent them. For example, in spite of current testing methods available for orthopedic concerns such as hip dysplasia, via the Orthopedic Foundation for Animals and PennHIP, hip problems can remain genetically recessive and multi-factorial; thus, no testing method is foolproof in

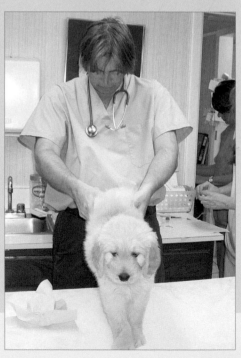

Although young puppies can be evaluated for hip health, the dog must be two years old to be certified as dysplasia-free.

preventing future occurences. Only by identifying DNA markers within individual animals, providing breeders with substantive "road maps" to compare prospective parental generational lineage charts, will successful outcomes in offspring be assured. We have not yet achieved such advancements to any great degree within the human world, much less in the animal kingdom, with only a small number of maladies identified through DNA thus far.

Not only have pure-bred gene pools been closed and "stagnating" in some perspectives, but some breeders have been selectively breeding to arbitrary standards, some of which are not necessarily based on anything scientific. For example, a broad-hipped, low-slung, straight-tailed Irish Setter could not possibly be indicative of ideal hip structure. Further, some breed standards require a small dome-shaped head and big ears, even though there is conjecture that such a head shape might in some cases indicate a genetic problem

akin to water on the brain (and a defect whereby the dog may even be missing part of the brain). Yet many breeders may struggle to breed this dome-shaped head into their lines for decades, regardless of the unknown potential for health complications. We need only to recall Monica (Joy) Parkin's earlier words when she was told by an all-breed dog-show judge that her winning show dog should still be bred in spite of the juvenile cataracts and von Willebrand's disease in his bloodline because he still had great "type" to pass on to future generations.

We now have a rather good idea of what hybrid vigor means in comparison to a "pure-bred" gene pool. We can see how this benefits our two wonderful parent breeds, the Poodle and the Golden Retriever, as their outstanding qualities can shine forth through hybrid vigor!

Another alluring element of these quality designer Goldendoodles is that they are still hard to come by. To some, owning a Goldendoodle before anyone else is a status symbol. Some want a Goldendoodle because their neighbor has one, and thus they feel that they need one too. Of course, Goldendoodle ownership, just like ownership of any dog, is a serious commitment that should not be entered into on a whim because a prospective owner is swept up in the designer-dog craze. If a person does decide that he is ready to devote the time to responsible ownership and properly caring for a Goldendoodle, these things are certain: Goldendoodles are absolutely adorable, unique, entirely individual, low-shedding, low-allergenic, loving, smart, easy to train, great-tempered, good with children and other pets, fantastic for therapy work and the list goes on!

Of all of the reasons for wanting a Goldendoodle, the number-one reason is, again, the hybrid vigor, with healthy lifespans projected for Goldendoodles bred carefully by knowledgeable breeders and who receive proper veterinary care throughout their lives.

The most prevalent health concerns shared by the parent breeds, the Poodle and the Golden Retriever, are primarily related to the hips and the eyes. Responsible breeders have the proper pre-breeding health-screening tests done and provide owners of their pups with health warranties that will cover any serious health concerns for a specified length of time. The time period varies among breeders but can sometimes be up to two years of age.

Generally speaking, Poodles and Golden Retrievers share no other major genetic health concerns. The certification of breeding stock based on hip x-ray evaluation by either the Orthopedic Foundation for Animals or the PennHIP program assures that dogs with bad hips will not be bred. The eye certification required of quality breeding stock comes from CERF (the Canine Eye Registration Foundation, located at Purdue University). Animals used for breeding should have their eyes tested annually by a qualified veterinary ophthalmologist.

Now that we know the origins of our Goldendoodles, how they are being developed and why they are so desirable as pets, let's move on to a detailed description of the Goldendoodle before we delve into the challenging maze of puppy acquisition in the age of the Internet.

CERF's up: all parent dogs must be evaluated annually for healthy eyes by a board-certified veterinary ophthalmologist like Dr. Marcia Aubin.

Handsome Rocky is swept away by the

Description of the
Goldendoodle

Universally accepted guide-
lines for standard Goldendoodles state that they
range in height from 21 to 24 inches (54 to 62 cm)
for males and 20 to 22.5 inches (51 to 58 cm) for
females. Males should weigh 55 to 75 pounds (25 to 34 kg)
and females 45 to 65 pounds (21 to 29 kg). Goldendoodles
sired by Miniature or Toy Poodles range in height from 13 to
21 inches (33 to 53 cm) and in weight from 25 to 45 pounds
(11 to 20.5 kg).

The term F_1, as we have already learned, refers to a
Goldendoodle puppy from a first mating or cross between a pure-
bred Golden Retriever and a pure-bred Poodle. It makes no
difference if the Poodle is the mother or the father, although in
the Miniature and Toy matings the Poodle is, of course, the stud,
via artificial insemination, and the Golden is the mother. By all
reports, all of these matings produce offspring that are
wonderful, warm, loving family pets with the desirable low-
shedding coats with minimal allergic reactions.

An F_{1B}, or backcross, is a first-cross Goldendoodle that is bred
back to a Poodle to produce Goldendoodle offspring that are
intended to have lower shedding potential than the first cross
(F_1), yet still have all of the endearing, lovable traits of the F_1
Goldendoodles.

phenomenon that is the Goldendoodle!

Goldendoodle pups adore nothing more than people, and that goes double for little people.

In some instances Goldendoodles are being bred to Goldendoodles, known as F_2 crosses or second-generation Goldendoodles. Owners are encouraged to seek out only the most experienced and devoted breeders for this type of Doodle, as increased dilution of the hybrid vigor phenomenon may occur.

Whatever the size or cross generation of a Goldendoodle, its temperament is one that comes from two parent breeds that adore people. The parent breeds are also both sporting, hunting, flushing and water-loving animals that are smart, loyal and easily trained, and enjoy lots of exercise, attention, socialization and family interaction. Doodles do not like to be left alone and will find innovative means to amuse themselves that can challenge even the most capable of owners and trainers, with chewing being the number-one concern. When considering placements for their puppies, Goldendoodle breeders look for potential owners who do not work long hours away from home or lead sedentary lifestyles.

All aboard for Doodle Island!

Doodling the time away

Goldendoodle
Puppy Acquisition

It is definitely the age of the Internet for the Goldendoodle, and it is worth taking a beginner's computer class to learn website exploration and basic email functions if you are not familiar with these. You might even want to corral your children, your grandchildren or a neighbor and make it a group project, which will be great fun for all!

The Internet simply is the number-one way to avoid pitfalls in finding your Goldendoodle puppy. However, this is only assured if you go about it the right way. After reading this book, the website to visit is the number-one international Goldendoodle website, www.goldendoodles.com, which was created and is maintained by a very talented and devoted Goldendoodle owner from Canada, Blue Sterling. Blue is the webmaster for this site, which was the first Goldendoodle website, and moderator of several online forums. She has an academic background in health science and a Bachelor of Arts degree in psychology. She and her husband live with four kids, three cats and two pet Goldendoodles in Ontario, Canada.

In 2000 in Ontario, there were no Labradoodles to be found online, but there were some "Golden Poos," which piqued Blue's interest. While waiting for her two "Golden Poos" to arrive from the breeder, Blue built the first Goldendoodle website and created online forums to pull together a community of Goldendoodle and

on a beautiful day with a beautiful dog.

Labradoodle owners and breeders. Supporting responsible ownership and responsible breeding practices, the Goldendoodle website sought to provide information to Doodle owners and future owners and to highlight the wonderful attributes of these hybrids. This site is a true celebration of the wonderful Goldendoodle in all its glory, including general resources, a database of coats and allergies, individual Doodle-and-owner pages, advice about how to read breeder sales contracts that protect both owner and puppy and more. A breeder displaying a Goldendoodles.com seal of approval is a proven, trustworthy breeder. Most importantly, the breeders listed at Goldendoodles.com are recommended by the owners of their dogs and share some like-minded philosophies that include health testing on hips and eyes and two-year health warranties. It is presently the most organized system in existence for regulating health and standards to keep the Goldendoodle from being ruined by poor breeding practices and opportunists who

You can find a Doodle like me through a dedicated breeder...don't settle for less.

have no regard for the dogs. The Goldendoodle website now has a small international team of people to manage it and help moderate the forums that Doodle owners and breeders use. It also provides links to other fine sites from its resource page.

Replete with knowledge and a central international database, files are maintained on breeders, both active and provisional, allowing prospective owners to make inquiries before deciding on a puppy from a breeder source. There are pages that discuss various aspects of what to look for and what to watch out for in a breeder, which will be discussed here also. Please read this advice carefully!

Some smaller websites may look reputable but require extreme caution as they may represent mediocre breeder cartels or other undisclosed special interests. It is recommended to use the tools found in this book and on Goldendoodles.com to help you recognize good breeders. Using the website of a breeder recommended by Goldendoodles.com is also a good place

THE BEST START IN LIFE

Ideally, if you chose a good breeder, your puppy will have been given the finest possible start in life:

- Born of fine-tempered, healthy parents who have been certified free of inherited diseases.
- Wormed and fully immunized for his age with state-of-the-art vaccines.
- Kept in the home or in a nursery, warm, clean and free of parasites.
- Fed the highest quality diet.
- Provided with veterinary supervision.
- Had dewclaws removed for safety.
- Given plenty of loving attention and provided with training experiences and socialization that coincide with his developmental stages.

Every day with a Goldendoodle is a cause for celebration. Today is Doodle dress-up day!

to start your search for your new Goldendoodle family member.

There are also several other websites that are good sources of information on the Goldendoodle, such as www.goDoodles.org for the New England Doodle Association (NEDA) and the International (formerly Indiana) Doodle Owners Group (IDOG) at www.IDOG.biz. No matter where you live, you will enjoy these two sites. For example, you can find and download interesting articles about IDOG and their activities on their website.

The NEDA forum, www.goDoodles.org, is visited by people from all over the world. Started by Kathryn Yamartino, the New England Doodle Association is a regional community of Doodle enthusiasts. The group is an outgrowth of a simple offer to establish an email list of Massachusetts Doodle owners participating on the Goldendoodles.com discussion forum. The group's mission, like that of most of the regional organizations, is to provide support and education for Doodle owners throughout its region and to promote responsible breeding practices. Along with its website and discussion forum, NEDA assists those looking for Doodles and those needing to place their Doodles in new homes and sponsors Doodle romps. Doodle romps are wonderful get-togethers for Doodles and their families. These gatherings are usually held at parks or farms where Doodles can run and safely play and, as the name implies, "romp." Children especially love taking their Doodles to their own special parties. Enterprising owners often pass out snacks for Doodles, such as platters of homemade carrot-cake treats good enough for all to eat. In the fall, some Doodles even wear their Halloween finery!

To summarize, the aforementioned online sites are the best places to find breeders and check out prospective puppies. The prices for quality Doodles now range from $1000 to $3500 or even more, plus additional charges if shipping is required.

A word here about the cost of your Doodle in the age of the Internet: we have read about the ways in which quality breeders are going to great expenses to expand the horizons for hybrid vigor in the Goldendoodle. Further, the Internet has increased the amount of time that goes into placing Doodles, with many hours of answering email inquiries and contacting prospective owners, which good breeders would have no other way. When you decide on a breeder, you will discover that most have deposit and/or waiting-list policies that vary from individual to individual. In general, though, refundable deposit policies are optimal in assuring that no puppy is locked into a home where he is no longer welcome. No caring breeder or owner would want this to occur.

Good breeding, which includes everything from the selection and actual mating of the parents, raising the puppies,

Meet IDOG

Here is a very interesting update from loyal Doodle enthusiast N. Beth Line, who shares about herself, the IDOG group and the group's current activities. First, a little about Beth:

• Owner of graphic design business since 1998
• Coordinator of the International Doodle Owners Group, formerly the Indiana Doodle Owners Group (IDOG, found at www.IDOG.biz)
• Member of K-9 Search and Rescue Unit
• Member of Paws and Think, Inc.
• Member of Association of Pet Dog Trainers (APDT)
• Supporter of Indiana Canine Assistant and Adolescent Network (ICAAN), a service-dog training program utilizing prisoners

N. Beth Line shares information about her activities and her IDOG group:

"With the support of the North American Labradoodle and Goldendoodle owners, I took a small team to Louisiana to work with pet rescue during the massive relief effort following Hurricane Katrina. We successfully helped them implement systems and methods to assure that the animals were properly cared for once they were rescued. Our team was also responsible for the care and protection of the fighting dogs, which required special handling. We helped coordinate and provided trouble-shooting and problem-solving for a facility that contained approximately 850 dogs. Our team also assisted with taking in rescue animals. One day we in took 800 dogs; the following days we were taking in 300 to 350 dogs a day.

"Prior to going to Louisiana for pet rescue, I, along with other members of the K-9 Search and Rescue Unit, were on standby to do recovery. We elected not to proceed because of the high risk of danger to the dogs from toxic slime.

"Presently, I am puppy-raising and training a Goldendoodle named Sherman. Sherman will go to his family in Hong Kong after he turns five months old. Due to the export regulations, the family could not have him sent when he was younger, so they asked me to care for him until he was old enough to travel. Here is a link to photo albums of our Doodles: http://www.picturetrail.com/nline.

"We established the IDOG site because we realized that people needed more information about Doodles. We were also highly concerned that we were going to start seeing backyard breeders pop up, and people were going to just run out and get any Doodle without knowing what it takes to care for a dog." The site was first developed to provide information to people in Indiana, but as Doodle popularity has grown, so has the need for reliable information that can be utilized by those around the world interested in Doodles.

"All of the breeders that are listed on the site have been personally interviewed, and we have personally gone to their homes to evaluate their programs. We established Doodle romps so that Doodle owners could meet each other and talk. We are also working on encouraging people to give their dogs jobs, especially therapy-dog work.

"Basically, we decided that we couldn't 'save the world,' but the least we could do was 'care for our own backyards.' Our site is about education, awareness and quality dogs for quality people."

Thanks to Beth from IDOG for sharing this information. For more about IDOG and Doodles, visit www.IDOG.biz. The IDOG site also has a link on its home page to the "Doodle Zoo" chat forum for those who want to ask questions, offer advice, share stories, etc.

He won't make your flowers grow, but he sure is cute!

placement of the puppies and after-sales support, is a service that mandates equivalent remuneration for hours and effort spent. The cost of your Goldendoodle is well worth the priceless return you receive for a wonderful puppy and good breeder support. It is an especially rewarding relationship when the owner and breeder are on the same page in putting a puppy's well-being first and foremost. On that note, if something does not work out in a puppy's new home, a good breeder invariably will want to rehome a dog of his breeding. In this situation, the owner should always return the dog to the breeder, never to a pound or shelter.

Let's now get back to our discussion about how to acquire your Goldendoodle puppy. A point of caution to add is that, while there are exceptions, most quality breeders do not need to advertise in newspapers, trade papers or online classified ads. Those "breeders" who do so might be trying to avoid the stringent breeding and health-warranty guidelines that are required in order to be listed as an approved breeder on the aforementioned websites. They may choose not to try to affiliate themselves with such sites because of the risk of negative owner feedback. So, if you find breeders and puppies that appeal to you through sources other than the reputable websites, get references on these breeders. Check them out through the trusted sites before buying! You can do this simply by going to a discussion board on Goldendoodles.com and typing in a question about your newly found breeder. Most always, you will be pleasantly relieved to know that someone knows and loves this breeder and his Goldendoodle! If not, consider yourself fortunate to be able to make an informed decision one way or another.

Nonetheless, it remains important that you ask a breeder for at least five references from owners of dogs from different litters, if possible, and that you ask to see documentation on the

"Thanks for everything, Mom! Good health, brains, charm...and have you seen how good-looking I am?"

parents' hip and eye clearances. You will also want to look over the breeder's sales contract and health warranties before purchasing a pup, and you should be provided copies of all documents at the time of purchase. You will know ahead of time, having read about contracts here or on Goldendoodles.com, how to read a contract and what "red flags" to look for, which will steer you away from the breeder. Such warnings include the contract's being void if you do not feed a certain type of food. Likewise, if there are too many exclusions in the contract, or if only "major" genetic diseases are covered, it likely indicates that the parents have not been screened or that the breeder has received many owner complaints in the past.

You should not have to pay extra for a health warranty. Generally, you should not have to adhere to any "gag" clauses, in which a breeder mandates your silence in order for you to be reimbursed for medical expenses or refunded for a puppy that became sick or died shortly after you received him. You should not have to return your puppy in order to be reimbursed for medical bills if it is your wish to keep him. A dishonest breeder may require the pup to be returned, thinking that you will have become attached to the pup and will not want to give him up, thus freeing the breeder of his obligation to reimburse for medical costs. To receive reimbursement from a good breeder, though, you will have to provide bona fide confirmation of veterinary costs.

Aside from all of the paperwork and references, you will want to meet the puppy's parents (at least the dam, as studs do not always belong to the breeder's kennel) if the breeder is within a reasonable distance from you. You will also want to know at what age the puppy will be released to you; puppies need adequate time with their dam and to be weaned before they leave for new homes.

You also need to know that posting questions about a breeder in an online discussion forum or chat room, which is open to all, can bring forth mixed feedback. Mediocre breeders may scour the forums in search of people wanting puppies and then send forth their soldiers to post glowing reviews. It has become a bit of a sham in terms of honest owner feedback, as those that are not approved breeders learn how to avoid stringent requirements.

On the other hand, if you already know that your breeder is a Goldendoodles.com-approved breeder and is established, it is a very good sign for you and your puppy. Remember, again, to look for the seal of approval that your breeder will display proudly, as the seal takes a lot of effort and many satisfied owners to earn. Still, it is important to ask questions and do your research, as many breeders are still on provisional lists, awaiting owner feedback from people just like you. You can offer feedback at any time by contacting the administrators of the sites.

It is of great importance that you plan ahead and be

Meeting the sire and dam of your Goldendoodle litter is absolutely ideal...and a whole lot of fun!

patient in your search for a breeder and puppy. Do not let thoughts of instant gratification take over your brain and rational thinking, as you may pay for this in heartbreak later. Some of the nice-looking, most intelligent-sounding websites can appear in several different forms and variations. All may link back to one very bad breeder who may have numerous complaints lodged against him with the reputable organizations and websites. So, again, be thorough in your research and use the tools you have learned about here and on Goldendoodles.com.

Ideally, you do want to find a puppy from a breeder who will be a resource to you throughout your Doodle's lifetime. The breeder should have one or both of the puppy's parents on his premises and should love and care for the parent(s) and the puppies as he would his own family members. The breeder's dogs should be provided with the best in veterinary care and quality of life.

Another thing to look for in a breeder is someone who will allow you to pick up your puppy when he is ready to go home. Some breeders are extremely selective about allowing visitors to meet the dam and her litter. Because of the popularity of Golden-doodles, there have been excessive visits to kennels by "gawkers" and "kennel-hoppers," meaning those who just want to see a Doodle. Since these people can put a breeder's puppies at a huge health risk, breeders have to screen potential buyers with utmost care. More than a few breeders have lost entire litters to deadly diseases such as parvovirus, which found its way into their kennels by having too many visitors. Potential owners should *never* visit more than one kennel per day.

Alternatively, you may be in a position where you need to have your puppy shipped to you. It is not an uncommon practice for Goldendoodle puppies sometimes to be shipped from reputable breeders. Most breeders who ship puppies can offer you excellent information on shipping practices and guidelines to ease your mind. If you need to have your dog shipped, ask your breeder in-depth questions about his protocol. When done appropriately, shipping proves to be an acceptable manner in which to acquire a Doodle puppy. On the other hand, if you have not done your homework, shipping can be a nightmare for you as well as for your puppy. One of the worst situations can be when an ill puppy is shipped back to the breeder when he should instead be getting medical attention. This is an example of satisfying the more inhumane concerns of money and contracts rather than putting the puppy's well-being first.

To reinforce the idea that it is not a good idea to rush into buying your Goldendoodle puppy, an owner has willingly offered to share with us an unfortunate experience, one of many that occur:

"I bought a sweet, beautiful, nine-week-old Doodle from a 'breeder' last week. The dog was shipped last Thursday. She is wonderful, intelligent and incredibly cute. I thought she would be the perfect antidote for my family's loss of our Golden Retriever to cancer recently.

"She is now lying in the animal hospital on IVs for possible parvovirus. From everything the vet is saying, the prognosis is poor. I am hoping for a miracle, but I would like to prepare for the worst. From the little time we had with her, I am convinced that 'Doodles rule.'

"The breeder is willing to send another [Goldendoodle] as if the first was a defective toaster, but claims no responsibility. She then tells me she had a litter wiped out last year. I spoke to other breeders through Goldendoodles.com who know of this breeder and did not have nice things to say about her.

"I will not accept another dog from this breeder at any cost. Again, I am hoping I don't have to, but this is the reality of it. I am now willing to wait, especially since it will take six months to feel confident I have rid my house of the virus."

Start Searching

Your safest ways to start your search for a Goldendoodle puppy are with a Goldendoodles.com-approved breeder, through links to the other reputable websites that we've discussed or by checking out breeders you find elsewhere with the tools you have learned about here.

This owner had gone off on his own to obtain a puppy, as he could not get a puppy right away from an approved Goldendoodles.com breeder. In explaining his foolhardy impatience, he stated that he was enthralled by finding a Doodle almost instantaneously from this so-called "breeder" and that he had been impressed by the breeder's website, which he now realizes is nothing more than slick. This is from an email from the owner to the breeder:

"I showed your email to the vet. I also spoke with the head vet at the 24-hour emergency/critical care animal hospital, a state-of-the-art facility. They did not agree with your treatment plan. I have spent several hours online researching the disease and speaking with reputable Doodle breeders throughout the country. It seems that you are very well known. Apparently there have been several similar situations in the past. They all have offered several suggestions.

"I am not interested in another pup from you. I am hoping and praying to save the one I have. Nor am I looking to cause you any problems or grief. I am expecting reimbursement for all of the medical bills, or a total refund if the puppy dies..."

The owner's battle with this breeder went on for months and was only settled half-heartedly, if at all. Files maintained at reputable Goldendoodle websites show more than a few similar occurrences with this breeder. Had the owner checked them first before buying, he would have known that the breeder had a "red flag" in the form of an ironclad contract that protected the breeder against just about everything with no concern for the owner and the Doodle puppies. So, while the Internet can be a wonderful tool, beware of the pitfalls!

Let's move on to preparing for your puppy's all-important first four months at home.

Congratulations!

In time, you will know how to use the Internet to find reputable puppy sources, will meet many new Doodle friends and owners-to-be on the discussion boards and will have learned so much about the canine world in general. Specifically, you will learn about Goldendoodles and how to raise them, care for them and keep them healthy, how to research to find a wonderful caring breeder who will be a source of help for your dog's lifetime and how to acquire a quality Doodle puppy. The work will be well worth it when your healthy and sound puppy is safely home with you.

With a Doodle in your life, it's always cuddle time.

A Goldendoodle puppy is an

Raising Your
Goldendoodle
Puppy

While you have been doing your research, working with a reputable breeder and waiting for your Goldendoodle puppy (the average waiting time for a quality puppy is 6 to 12 months), you will also have had plenty of time to check out local veterinarians, meet some dog trainers in your area and peruse some recommended training manuals, as well as puppy-proof your house. These are all necessary steps in preparing for the arrival of your new Goldendoodle puppy.

We will begin by discussing veterinary concerns. You will want to find a veterinarian with whom you are comfortable, who recommends pet insurance options, as this writer does, and who offers emergency calling hours and/or has emergency contingency alternatives at all times with an emergency hospital or vet with whom you also are comfortable. Some vets may offer boarding, training and house-call options. You want a vet who is forward-thinking regarding occasional holistic advancements in diet and treatments and believes in continuing education for vets and veterinary assistants (who often do many treatments on your pet unassisted). If your pet needs to stay overnight, you want to make certain that he will be monitored appropriately.

You want a veterinary office that appears clean, as canine diseases can be highly contagious, especially to new puppies, and

all-natural "pick me up."

Veterinarians are meeting new Goldendoodles every day—aren't they lucky?

an office that is friendly and is easily accessible in emergency situations for your pet. When taking a new puppy in for his first check-up, it is wise never to put him on the floor or let him be handled by strangers. Generally, new puppies are not fully immune for four months or until an entire series of shots is complete, so they should not be exposed to dog parks, pet stores, highway rest stops, kennels, grooming salons and other places where lots of other dogs congregate and relieve themselves.

Generally, puppies receive their first temporary shots while still with their breeder, and then they visit the vet with their new owners for their subsequent permanent shots. Puppy-shot schedules and protocol may vary according to region, vet and individual puppy, so consult your vet and breeder.

Permanent shots may be given over a period of time between 6 and 16 weeks of age, with the shots being given approximately 3 weeks apart, as a series to cover the period of time during which puppies begin to lose their maternal immunity.

Puppies receive their first immunity from their mother's milk during the first few days of life. There are many variables to this, such as litter size and order of birth, so some puppies may have more immunity than others. There is therefore a wide time frame given to all puppies to cover them whether they received more or less immunity from their mother. Puppy shots are very important and protect from diseases such as parvovirus, distemper, parainfluenza, leptospirosis, hepatitis, coronavirus and rabies. You must adhere to the vaccination schedule set forth by your vet; in fact, the rabies shot must be given by law. The first rabies shot is good for one year, and the next shot is usually a two- or three-year vaccine, depending on where you live.

Your vet will put you on an appropriate schedule for your puppy's shots as well as booster shots throughout your dog's life. Annual check-ups are recommended to monitor the dog's overall health as well as to get a supply of flea, tick and heartworm protection. An annual heartworm test is necessary in order for the vet to prescribe another year's worth of heartworm preventative. Many heartworm preventatives also protect against other dangerous internal parasites. The vet should examine a stool sample from your adult dog annually to check for worms and parasites. A puppy should have his stool examined at least two or three times during his first year.

You will want to discuss additional vaccinations for kennel cough and Lyme disease; your vet may or may not recommend these depending on your living environment and lifestyle. You will want to discuss elective procedures, such as microchipping or tattooing your Doodle puppy for identification purposes.

Discuss spaying/neutering with your breeder and vet. Most reputable Goldendoodle

A four-month-old pup
follows his two-month-
old friend...how quickly
they grow!

breeders require most Goldendoodle puppies to be spayed (females) or neutered (males) once they reach the appropriate age, although some are now being spayed and neutered by their breeders before being placed with owners. Breeders are very serious that you spay or neuter your pet. The owner who lies about his intentions for his Goldendoodle puppy and then abuses the breeder's spay/neuter requirements (which will be clearly spelled out in the sales contract) has already proven that he is poorly qualified to be a Goldendoodle owner, much less to breed his dog and raise puppies.

There are some breeders who do make provisions for placing puppies in approved breeding homes, so you should be honest about your intentions from the outset. If you are planning to become a breeder or to have a litter of puppies for your family members, do it honestly; do not lie about future breeding plans. If you are dishonest,

you are looking for trouble and will lose the respect of an entire network of Doodle breeders and owners. Everyone in the Doodle community frowns upon such dishonest measures as much as, if not more than, the reputable breeders who are being taken advantage of.

Neutering/Spaying

Some facts you should know:
- A non-spayed female has an increased chance of acquiring breast cancer during her first or second heat cycle.
- It is a myth that females benefit from one heat and a litter.
- Females should be spayed before their first heat.
- Males risk testicular cancer and unwelcome behaviors if not neutered.
- Neuter/spay responsibly, which usually means before the pup reaches six months of age. Follow the advice of your vet and breeder.

A WORD ABOUT DIET

Your puppy's size can double between 8 and 16 weeks, and the puppy keeps on growing lickety-split until about 9 months of age, when his growth starts to slow down.

A high-quality dog food recommended by your breeder or your vet is important. Even when fed properly, your puppy still can be prone to loose-stool issues with any changes in diet or additions of new snacks or chew toys. Sometimes a day or two of serving ground chicken and rice and withholding treats can settle an upset tummy. Switching to a more natural holistic diet can help some puppies, but for other puppies this type of diet is too rich.

Once you find the right food, things will be fine. Anytime you have to change your Goldendoodle's food, gradually mixing less of the old food with more of new food enables a smooth transition. Your vet's guidance is invaluable in all things, and

"I'll drink to that!" Keep the water clean, fresh and flowing.

that good breeder that you chose so carefully will be right there with you as well.

It is equally important to discuss what puppies should *not* eat. Puppies are very oral and will put almost anything in their mouths. It is important to keep your puppy away from things that can cause him harm if ingested. For example, mulch can contain toxic cocoa hulls, sticks can splinter and get stuck in the throat, plastic bags can get stuck in the back of the throat or over the puppy's head, cat litter can block airways and gravel can lead to stomach blockage. The eating of socks or similar items also can cause life-threatening bowel blockages if left unattended. Another household danger is antifreeze, which is palatable to animals but toxic. Additionally, there are certain foods that are toxic to dogs, among them choc-olate, nuts, grapes, raisins, onions and significant quanti-ties of garlic.

Mealtime is every dog's favorite time, and Doodles are no exceptions.

Consistency in training makes all the difference. Your Doodle will learn which door is his "bathroom" door.

TRAINING

Another aspect of puppy raising to discuss is training. A professional trainer certainly can be a big help not just in teaching your puppy but also in helping you prepare and care for your puppy. Hopefully during your months of waiting for your puppy, you have found a wonderful private trainer to talk with before your puppy comes home. This trainer will advise you about puppy-proofing your home, getting the right-sized crate (the crate you get at the outset should be big enough for the adult-sized Doodle to stand up and turn around in) and suitable toys. Durable rubber toys filled with treats will surely keep a dog busy, as will knotted rope toys, which will not break young teeth. Fuzzy things, snuggly things and things that roll are also fun, but make sure that the toy is always bigger than the puppy's mouth and has no parts that can break off and be swallowed. Only approved pet toys, not children's toys, are good for puppies, as is flat rawhide, not the compressed variety.

Puppies like to chew, so stainless steel food and water bowls are best because plastic bowls can be chewed. You can also run into the same problem with fabric crates, so stick with the wire or fiberglass crates with divider panels that you can remove as the puppy grows. A crate that has a door both on the end and on the side gives you options regarding the direction in which you can place the crate in your home.

The trainer and breeder may suggest where you should put your crate; the kitchen and family room are wise choices. Crate training is excellent for your puppy. It is a very successful method of potty training; further, the crate keeps your puppy safe when you cannot be around to watch him and also gives him his own quiet-time space.

It is important not to abuse crate training by leaving a puppy in his crate longer than recommended. A good rule of thumb to

If the crate is a fun and cozy place, your pup will learn to love it and will want to keep it clean.

determine how many hours a pup can be left in the crate is to use his age in months plus one. For example, if your puppy is two months old, he can most likely stay in his crate no longer than three hours before needing to be taken outside to go potty. Plus, he will also need to get some exercise and training. Never expect your puppy to stay crated for more than five hours, unless he's sleeping.

Let's talk about potty training in conjunction with crate training. It really is very simple: your puppy does not want to have potty accidents any more than you want him to. He does not like to "go" where he eats, sleeps or plays. That is why you should keep him in a confined area for his first few days at home. Many puppies raised by good breeders go to their new homes on their way to being paper-trained, crate-trained and house-trained (another benefit of that good breeder you have researched, chosen and waited for!). Your trainer will also give you a schedule for taking your puppy out: first thing every morning, after

naps, after playtimes, etc., and always to the same spot that you have chosen as his relief area.

When you take the puppy outside, do not play with him first. Take him outside immediately after taking him out of the crate, lead him to his spot and, after he follows your "Go potty" command successfully, you then praise him for a job well done. Anytime a puppy wakes up from a nap, the very first thing he wants to do is go potty, so again out he goes.

The key to successful potty training is consistency in feeding schedules and no dietary changes, which can cause loose stools. Whether you feed two or three times a day, always feed him at the same times and take him out shortly thereafter. In the beginning, remove the puppy's water two to three hours before his bedtime to decrease his need to go out in the middle of the night. Always take your puppy out through the same door, to the same potty spot, using the same "Go potty" command. When he's

Crate Facts

In the wild, canines prefer to sleep and raise their young in dens, which are small, enclosed areas where the dogs feel safely surrounded on all sides and are able to sense intruders approaching. At very early ages, puppies learn to relieve themselves outside the den, as that is where they smell the deposits of other dogs, which attracts them to that location.

Using a crate for your pup during house-training recreates this instinctual behavior, giving your pup the security he desires and teaching him to contain himself when you cannot be there to take him to his relief area. As he cannot move around much, he won't need to relieve himself as often. Using the crate will help you gain control of his scheduling as well as help you teach Junior to potty on command, for you will know that he will definitely have to relieve himself the moment you let him out of his crate.

Don't be frightened of using a crate...your puppy won't be.

Lead him to his favorite tree. The rest will come naturally.

done relieving himself, offer praise and maybe a treat and then take him back inside for some playtime and affection.

Confinement and supervision are important for both training and safety purposes. In addition to a crate, many owners like to block doorways with baby gates to keep puppy in certain rooms and out of others. However, avoid the old-fashioned accordion-style wooden gates, as a puppy can get his head stuck in between the slats. The same goes for deck railings; be careful of how far apart the slats are spaced. Metal identification tags that hang down can get caught on things like slats, fences or curtain cords; choose tags that attach close to the collar or slide right onto the collar. Avoid picket fences lower than 5 feet high or collars on your dog that do not break when stressed, as tragic endings can happen if a dog is caught on a fence by his collar when he jumps up.

Think again of your puppy as no different than a human baby and perhaps even in more need of a watchful eye. A pup's inquisitiveness and activity level are high when it comes to exploring his

A happy, attentive Doodle makes training time fun.

Once he has learned the sit, you can progress to teaching the down exercise, using gentle encouragement and praise.

environment indoors and out. Therefore, one of the first and most important things to teach your puppy is to come to you when called. Have your puppy follow you around and use a very animated, higher-pitched tone to tell him to "Come." When he does, a small training treat will reward this behavior and encourage him to repeat it. Also, you can put your puppy on a leash, stand a few feet away while holding the leash and, in your happy higher voice, tell him to "Come." Tug him gently to you while squatting down with your arms wide open, that's a great reason for the puppy to want to come to you!

Next, you may want to work on "Sit." You will learn this in a puppy class or you can practice on your own with your puppy. Hold a training treat just over the puppy's forehead as you command him to "Sit" and move the treat toward his back, and puppy will lean back and end up in the sitting position. Then praise the puppy and offer an extra treat!

A procedure for redirecting inappropriate behavior in a young puppy, similar to how his mother would correct the puppy still in the litter, is to first get the puppy's attention by using a low-pitched, serious voice with an "Ahhh!" or "No," which will startle the puppy. This will cause him to stop what he is doing and look to you for further direction, at which time you would provide an alternative behavior that acts as a distraction from the unacceptable behavior. This can work if, for example, the puppy is nipping at your hand, chewing your table leg or biting the cat's tail. When puppy changes to an acceptable behavior, such as chewing on a toy you have just offered, say "Good puppy" in a nice, high-pitched, happy voice and reward the puppy with praise or a treat.

Puppies understand three different tones generally: high, which is similar to littermates and is used to motivate; medium, which is like an ordinary bark and is a tone you would use for a calm

Coming to you should always result in something pleasant for your dog.

Teaching the heel command is well worth the effort. Walks with your Doodle should be enjoyable, not a struggle.

Puppy-Proofing Tips

As you puppy-proof your home, here are some additional things to remember. You should keep the following out of puppy's reach: electrical cords, tablecloths, houseplants (some can be toxic; look online for a complete list) and household cleaners. Keep your cupboards locked with your puppy, as you would do with a human toddler.

Other things dangerous to all dogs, puppy or adult, big or small, in addition to things we've already mentioned are cheese in large quantities (dogs can be lactose intolerant), acetaminophen, lead, zinc, tick and flea collars, bees, fire ants, toilet bowl cleaners (in the water and out), glue, window cleaners, ammonia, bleach, mistletoe, macadamia nuts, apple seeds, peach and apricot pits, philodendrons, poinsettias, mums, asparagus ferns, gasoline, kerosene, acetone, paint thinner and more. Use your common sense! Keep these poison control contacts handy:

ASPCA ANIMAL POISON CONTROL
(888) 426-4435 (credit card charge)
1-900-443-0000 (phone bill charge)
www.aspca.org/apcc

ANIMAL POISON HOTLINE
(888) 232-8870 (credit card charge)
www.animalpoisonhotline.com

command; and the lower tones, similar to a growl that a mother uses to warn her puppies when she is tired of inappropriate behavior. It is fascinating to watch how a loving canine mother interacts with her litter as the pups grow and she disciplines them. There are many obvious advantages to leaving the pups with their dam for a full eight weeks. It can have lasting negative socialization effects if a puppy is removed too early from his mother or his littermates.

Moving on, let's talk about temperament testing. The majority of Goldendoodles are still picked by breeders for owners. Owners invariably ask for calm, well-mannered, non-dominant puppies. Temperament testing in puppies less than eight weeks is highly variable because puppies are still very much growing and developing. A skillful trainer not only can assist a new owner in setting up a good household routine for a puppy but also can begin temperament evaluation to modify early training techniques for the individual puppy. In this way, all Doodles can grow up

to have the most ideal temperaments and behavior for their owners.

Some temperament tests that might be used with a puppy by a trainer, owner or breeder are the jingling of keys and the clapping of hands to see how the puppy reacts, and the rubbing of puppy's tummy and the touching of his mouth for temperament and dominant/ submissive issues.

The best time for puppies to form socialization skills that last throughout their lives is between 3 and 12 weeks of

Every Doodle litter deserves a round of applause!

age, according to Karla S. Rugh, DVM, Ph.D., as cited in *Start Off Right.* She recommends exposing your puppy to as "many different individuals (humans, dogs and other animals), situations and experiences as possible." Touch your puppy's tummy, paws and ears; attach a lightweight leash to his collar and let him drag it around the house to get used to walking outside with you; let him play with healthy adult dogs; introduce him to older people, people with sunglasses, children, etc.; let him see kids on bikes and scooters; take him on leash to watch a children's soccer game; teach him to sit on leash calmly as cars go by or as the vacuum cleaner is on; take him for rides in the car; introduce him to cats or show him horses or cows in a field. The list is endless. This period of time is the optimal time for socialization.

Let's get physical: notice how dogs use their paws and mouths at play.

A word of advice regarding trainers and techniques: with all of the training books and methods available, stick with one good trainer who uses a method based on kindness, encouragement and positive reinforcement, not punishment. Get a copy of *Puppy Training* by Charlotte Schwartz for a detailed week-by-week primer for your growing Doodle. Further, puppy kindergarten and then advanced training classes are excellent ways to train your puppy. As long as there is consistency, affection, fun and teamwork in training your Goldendoodle puppy, you will have a well-mannered puppy and will figure out a common-sense training method that works for you.

Do not make yourself or your puppy neurotic by trying to adhere to training manuals as if they were carved in stone. This is a time when you should also enjoy and play with your puppy appropriately, which a good trainer can also guide you in doing. For example, Martha Francis, the

Some balls are for chasing... some are for chewing.

owner of Fetch Dog Training (www.fetchdogtraining.com) in the Boston, Massachusetts area states that Doodle puppies can be "mouthy" due to the Golden Retriever's and Poodle's both being oral breeds. It's important that you don't sit on the floor and play with your puppy with your hands, as this encourages mouthiness. It is better to always approach your pup with a chew toy and play fetch games to get him "object-oriented" from the start. Further, she advises to "never let your puppy chase

"Welcome to our home!"
Goldendoodle Guy is a gracious host.

Take the lead! Get started with your Doodle pup's training early on.

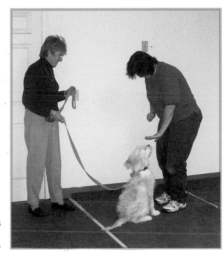

At puppy training classes, both owners and dogs get an education.

and nip your children. Your children are not play toys and you always need to supervise their interaction. It's too easy for your puppy to see them as littermates and get too rough with them."

Your trainer can advise you on the best time for puppy kindergarten classes, where you will meet lots of other dogs and owners. Your wonderful Goldendoodle puppy will probably win an award for being one of the brightest students in the class.

For families in which both parents work and the kids are at school all day, a well-trained Doodle will enjoy spending time at one of the many doggie daycare centers now available. Many have live web cameras where owners can check on their Doodles during the day from their office computers and watch them play.

To summarize the main aspects and the importance of your puppy's all-important first four months with you,

included here is some advice from a brilliant trainer who has worked with hundreds of Doodles. You should look for similar credentials in trainers when choosing one for your Goldendoodle puppy, as all trainers are not alike. Meet Martha Francis of Fetch Dog Training, which offers group classes, puppy kindergarten, graduate classes and private training in homes in the western suburbs of Boston. She is a lifelong dog owner of a wide variety of breeds, relates well to people and dogs and humorously decorates her business communications with a quote from Andy Rooney on dog training: "If dogs could talk, it would take a lot of fun out of owning one." She worked in the corporate world for many years, training dogs on the side, but left her corporate job in 2000 to devote her full attention to her number-one passion of dog training.

Martha's credentials are outstanding. She is a Certified Pet Dog Trainer, is a member of the Association of Pet Dog Trainers, has a BA degree from Boston University and an MBA from Harvard University Extension and has studied with two of the best British dog trainers, John Rogerson and Dr. Ian Dunbar, as well as many American trainers and behaviorists.

Learn new things and make new friends...training classes offer many benefits.

Never underestimate the power of a treat!

MARTHA FRANCIS OFFERS THESE FIRM BELIEFS ABOUT GOLDENDOODLES, FROM HER FIRST-HAND OBSERVATIONS:

- Like all other dogs, Goldendoodles need thoughtful and careful breeding to develop sound health and temperament.

- As Goldendoodles are one of the most popular "designer dogs," many irreputable breeders have gotten in on the action and are breeding dogs with terrible health and temperaments.

- As you would with any dog, choose your breeder carefully. Most people don't realize just how important the first eight weeks of a puppy's life really are. If raised properly, your eight-week-old puppy can arrive nearly house-trained, well socialized and able to handle being left alone for periods of time.

- Goldendoodles are very easy to train. They seem quite willing to please focus well and really enjoy the training experience. I have not seen any "stubborn" Goldendoodles. There is no limit to what they can accomplish.

"Crate? What crate?"

Making a splash comes naturally to the Goldendoodle!

Martha Francis generously shares the following tips on training your Doodle:

- The best gift you can give your Goldendoodle puppy is to train him well. This is a dog with which you will live and share your house for the next 12 to 15 years. Start training on the day you bring your puppy home. It is so much easier than waiting, and Goldendoodles are like little sponges that just want to soak it all in. Set your rules right away, and your puppy will follow them. Just be calm, patient, fair and consistent.

- House-training is also about surface discrimination, not just inside/outside. If you can prevent accidents in the house on your floors and carpets, and the puppy only has the opportunity to go to the bathroom on dirt or grass, it will become his preferred surface for elimination. Drive the message home by giving the pup a treat within two seconds of his finishing his business. Always take your puppy outside on a leash so you can be right there to praise him and give him a treat so he gets the message. If you wait to give him a treat until you take him back indoors, he'll think he's being rewarded for coming inside.

- Crates are not cruel! The crate is a valuable aid to housebreaking and a sanctuary for your pup to get away from it all. As long as your puppy is getting lots of exercise, socialization with people and interaction with you, crating him is fine when you can't keep an eagle eye on him. All puppies need to learn that being calm and quiet is a part of their lives, too.

• Don't give your puppy too much freedom. Keep your puppy gated in the kitchen with his crate open as his house-training improves. Once he is completely house-trained in the kitchen, you can introduce him to one new room, perhaps the family room. Start feeding him in that room and doing your obedience training there so he considers it as a new part of his territory and will be less likely to soil there.

• Socialize your puppy now. If he isn't fully immunized, have him meet dogs that you know are healthy and fully immunized. Have him meet lots of people. Take your puppy everywhere: outdoor cafés, walks around town, school to pick up the kids, soccer games, etc. Socialization is not just about meeting other puppies: it's about the puppy's getting used to the entire world around him without being frightened. He should react calmly to traffic noises, car rides, cats, horses, motorcycles, trucks, bicycles, joggers, baby carriages, wheelchairs, thunderstorms, toddlers, noisy teenagers, etc.

Blondes have more fun!

Goldendoodles can be fairly large, so discouraging pulling on the leash from the outset is good with any puppy. Pulling is a hard habit to break if it's allowed to happen. Whenever the puppy pulls, stand still and say "Easy" and wait until the pup slackens up on the leash before proceeding. This can be tedious work, so when owners don't have the time, a head collar can work as a management tool. There are also harnesses available that work well. Just remember that these are management techniques only for when you just need to walk the pup and don't have the time or patience to train him on his regular collar.

Thanks to Martha Francis for these special hints!

"Ease on down the road" with your Goldendoodle.

RING MY BELL

Something that is particularly fun about the world of Goldendoodles is how they like to ring bells in order to go outside to the chosen spots to which they have been trained for their potty needs. Holly Haringa, an experienced owner of delightful brother and sister Goldendoodles, Fiona and Finnegan Doodle, shares her training advice with you:

"For bells, they are sleigh-bell types that can be purchased at a craft store. Hang them on a ribbon from the doorknob low enough for dog to reach with his nose. Train the dog to ring the bells with his nose so as not to scratch the door with pawing. Try to make the reward going outside, not treats. If you use treats, the dog will associate ringing the bell with getting a treat and will ring more often. It is important when teaching this to let the dog out every time he rings the bells. At first this may be a game for the dog, but he will soon settle down and ring the bells when he actually needs to go out."

As we close this chapter, the author hopes that you too will get bells for your new Goldendoodle puppy and also gives you this promise:

"Be still and listen. Like wind chimes all across America and abroad, on breezes high and low, shiny Goldendoodle noses, one by one, nuzzle bells that herald forth:

"'We are here! With eyes that shine like angels' souls! Love us as we love you! We are center stage now, our act just beginning, our play eternal!'"

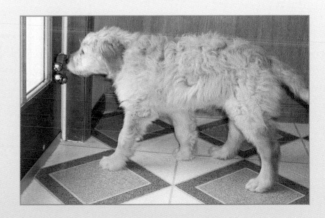

The chimes ring out the news: Goldendoodles are here!

How do you make your Goldendoodle slicker?

Goldendoodle coat types can

range from very from soft and wavy fluff to tight and curly, and can be 4 to 8 inches long. The coat should be brushed and combed daily or groomed regularly by a professional. There are many different grooming techniques, but be sure to leave some feathering around the face, which allows the Goldendoodle to distinguish himself wherever he goes. Washing your Doodle only when necessary is recommended, as bathing too frequently can dry out the coat and skin. To dry the Doodle, you can use a blow dryer, but just be sure to use a low heat setting and hold the dryer at a comfortable distance from the dog. Always diffuse the warm air with your hand and fluff the hair as you dry so that you do not burn your Goldendoodle's skin. Another helpful bath hint: you may also want to purchase a bottle of skunk deodorizer at a pet-supply store and keep it handy at all times...just in case!

Owners with very active lifestyles prefer grooming shorter coats in warmer months, as the shorter coats are easier to care for when the dog is doing more swimming and romping about. Other owners prefer the longer coats and commit themselves to daily combing and coats left *au naturel*.

With a slicker brush, of course!

Brush your Doodle daily, especially if he has a heavier coat.

What'll it be...curly or wavy?

Grooming rakes are ideal tools for dealing with the thicker mats that sometimes can form close to the skin in heavier Doodle coats.

A word to the wise for those who use professional groomers: be sure to tell your groomer precisely how you wish your Doodle to look. Many groomers do not know exactly what to do with a Goldendoodle, and you don't want to leave your dog at the grooming salon only to return and find him completely shaved down.

Your Doodle's nails should be trimmed as needed; it's easiest to include this in the grooming routine along with his brushing and combing. You can do this yourself at home with canine nail clippers purchased at a pet-supply shop, or you can ask your vet or groomer to clip your dog's nails. If you are trimming your dog's nails, be careful to only clip away a little at a time and keep a supply of styptic powder on hand in case the "quick" (vein that runs inside the nail) gets cut accidentally, which will cause bleeding. It is best to have someone like a groomer or your vet show you the proper way to trim your dog's nails before you attempt it yourself.

Part of a Goldendoodle's regular grooming should be caring for his ears. A common household recipe for an ear-cleaning formula is using a solution of one-half vinegar and one-half water. This is to keep an acidic environment in the ears to prevent the formation of yeast infections. Doodles are prone to these ear infections, especially when swimming and in hotter months. This simple solution can be made by buying a bottle of white vinegar, pouring half of it into a spray bottle, and then filling both bottles with water of

equal measure to the vinegar. You will then have one bottle to use for ear cleaning and a spray bottle to use for cleaning up any urine accidents on the floor or rugs, as white vinegar neutralizes urine. The solution can also be used to clean puppy paw prints off of glass.

Hypoallergenic soft baby

"I don't look this good by accident."

You don't need a fancy salon to keep your Doodle looking like a million bucks.

wipes are also good for external cleaning of the ear canals; you should never probe into the ear canals, as this can injure the ears. Deep cleaning of the ear canals is for the vet only. Repeated ear discharge requires veterinary care, as it can indicate bacterial infections or mite infestation.

Hypoallergenic baby wipes can be used for more than just the ears. As part of a daily grooming ritual, you can use these wipes to clean your puppy's private areas and around his tummy; young puppies, both male and female, are prone to squatting and wallowing somewhat in their urine. Wiping these areas of your pup's body daily prevents the formation of staph infections or pustules. These can look like little white pimples or big red bumps on their tummies, or redness around the urethras on males or vaginas on females. These

infections require veterinary attention. Also, trim the hair that can grow quite long in the genital areas as this can prevent dried urine on long hair from causing infection. If you prefer, you can ask your vet or groomer to do this. Always be sure not to clip any skin.

In applicable months, appropriate flea and tick preventive medications, obtained from your vet, should be applied per the instructions A daily check for ticks and fleas is still advised, as no preventative is 100% effective in keeping these nasty parasites off of your pet. Flea and tick collars should not be used on young puppies and may not be recommended for your Doodle at all; ask your vet about the safest preventives for all stages of your Golden-doodle's life. Also ask your vet about the vaccine for the dangerous tick-borne illness, Lyme disease.

What could be more fun than one Goldendoodle?

Your Goldendoodle can

partake in nearly any activity you wish. The myriad abilities of both parent breeds combine in a Doodle whose potential is sky-high! The Goldendoodle's skills, trainability and versatility enable him to assist others, to reach high levels of success in many areas of the dog sport and to do many things with his owners just for fun.

Goldendoodles are being used successfully as guide dogs for the blind, hearing dogs for the deaf and assistance dogs for the handicapped. Their intelligence, ability to learn and willingness to please their owners make them well suited to these tasks, and Goldendoodle breeders are happy to report when dogs from their lines are accepted into training programs. Further, the low-allergenic properties of the Goldendoodle's coat opens up possibilities for those who need canine helpers but had not been able to have them due to problems with allergies.

There are different types of training programs for future assistance dogs. Often, a prospect is raised by a volunteer family at home, where he is socialized and obedience-trained according to the procedures and rules of the assistance-dog organization. The pup's upbringing is monitored and, upon reaching a certain age, he is returned to the organization to

How about a matched pair!

receive specialized training in assistance work and eventually be paired up with a human partner. Another training period takes place as the dog learns to work with his new owner and the owner learns how to communicate with the dog. It's a lengthy

Now the family is really complete.

and involved process, but a rewarding one for Goldendoodles, who love the challenges and love working with and for people. To have a job to do and an adoring human to do it for—what could be better for this doting and dutiful Doodle?

Goldendoodles are always eager to help with chores.

Just add water and watch the fun begin!

COMPETITIVE SPORTS

Goldendoodles have the potential to excel in many types of canine competition, including obedience, agility, flyball and more. They can attend only training, practice and fun matches held by the American Kennel Club, as the Goldendoodle is not AKC-recognized and thus cannot earn AKC awards and titles. However, there are plenty of events held by clubs that allow all dogs to compete, regardless of breed or mix. In these cases, Goldendoodles have the opportunity to win certificates, awards and titles offered by the clubs. The United Kennel Club (UKC) is a national club in the US that has a registry for pure-bred dogs, but allows dogs of all breeds, including mixed breeds, to compete in its performance events. You likely also will be able to find an "all-breed" or "all-dog" club in your area that places no restrictions on the dogs that can compete. Also check with your local kennel club, who may allow your

Goldendoodle in matches. Now let's explore some of the popular areas of the dog sport.

Although exact exercises and rules will vary depending on the hosting club or organization, obedience competition typically encompasses three levels of difficulty: Novice, Open and Utility. Obedience-trial championships can be earned once all of the levels are completed successfully, which is quite a feat! Following are explanations of some of the exercises that are generally found in obedience competition. Before you enter an obedience trial, you will familiarize yourself with the specific exercises and requirements of the club hosting the competition.

At each level of competition, there are usually two sets of exercises: the first for one dog-and-handler team only, and the second for a group of dogs and their handlers. At the easiest, or Novice, level, the individual exercises include heeling both on and off leash, a figure-8 on leash while heeling, performing a stand/stay while the judge walks around and touches the dog and performing a sit/stay followed by a recall (come) from 30 feet away. A "finish" is often required. To perform the finish, the handler instructs the dog to get into the heel position. The dog then places himself at his handler's left side, either by going behind the handler or by swinging around in front of the handler (this is according to the individual dog's preference, which the owner should be familiar with).

For group exercises, there are never more than 12 dogs and their handlers in the ring at the same time. In the Novice level, the dogs are lined up on one side of the ring, side by side, about 2 feet away from each other. The owners face the opposite end of the ring with their dogs sitting in the heel position. At the judge's instruction, the handlers give their dogs the stay command and then walk to the other side of the ring and turn to face their dogs. The dogs must remain in the sit/stay for a full 60

seconds, after which the judge tells the handlers to return to their dogs. This exercise is repeated in a down/stay; the dogs must hold this position for three minutes. Breaking from the proper position in either exercise gets a dog disqualified from the class.

The Open level is the next level of difficulty. Similar exercises are required, yet everything must be performed off leash. Several more difficult exercises are introduced as well; one of these is the drop on recall, in which the dog is told to stay at one end of the ring while his handler goes to the other end. The judge signals the handler to do a recall (come). When the dog is halfway to the handler, the handler must signal for the dog to lie down. After the dog lies down, the judge gives the okay to complete the recall. The dog should come to the handler and sit in front of him, after which the judge signals for the finish. Quite a process for just one exercise!

Another Open-level exercise is the retrieve on the flat. The handler gives the stay command and then throws a dumbbell at least 20 feet in front of him and the dog. The judge signals the handler to send the dog. At the handler's instruction, the dog must retrieve the dumbbell and return to sit in front of the handler, holding the dumbbell in his mouth until the judge's signal, upon which the dog drops the dumbbell into his handler's hand. This exercise also ends with a finish.

The Open level also includes the broad jump. Different clubs have different approaches to this exercise. One way is that the handler stands beside the jump as the dog goes over the jump, sits in front of the handler and then returns to heel position. Another way is that the handler is on the other side of the jump, facing the dog. The handler signals for the dog to jump over, and the dog sits in front of the handler after completing the jump.

There are group exercises in the Open level; these are similar to those required at the Novice level and differ only in that the dogs must remain in a sit/stay for three minutes and a down/stay for five minutes with the handlers out of sight. This requires a dog to really ignore distractions, as there is so much going on at obedience shows. Aside from the other handlers and dogs, both in the ring and outside the ring, there are plenty of spectators. The dogs also must have faith that their handlers will return.

The Utility level is next. It is worth mentioning that a dog must progress through the levels in order of difficulty; he cannot compete in Utility if he has not already met the requirements of both Novice and Open. However, when training your Goldendoodle, do not feel restricted. A Goldendoodle may be competing at the Novice level, but he will stay motivated and interested if you teach him more difficult exercises in addition to what he needs to know for his current level of competition. Plus, he will be well prepared for the higher levels once he is qualified for them.

Don't forget the "retriever" in your Doodle's Golden lineage.

The Utility level is quite interesting to watch, as many of the cues are delivered visually. One exercise is the heel, and the handler instructs the dog with only visual cues. Upon near-completion of the heel, the dog is left in a stand/stay while the handler walks forward another 20 feet and stops. Upon the judge's okay, the handler signals the dog to the heel position, again with a visual cue. Other Utility exercises include scent discrimination, object discrimination and directed jumping.

In scent discrimination, the dog must retrieve both a leather and a metal object containing the handler's scent. The objects with the handler's scent are placed among 11 other identical, but unscented, objects. In object discrimination, there are three identical gloves laid out in a line. The judge tells the handler which glove the dog must retrieve, and the handler conveys this to the dog through signals. The dog must pick the correct glove, return with the glove, sit in front the handler, drop the glove on command and perform a finish. You can see how the exercises get more difficult and more precise with each level.

There are several parts to directed jumping. The first is the "go out," in which the dog must go to the opposite side of the ring from his handler and then turn and sit to face the handler. There are two jumps in the ring, a bar jump and a flat-panel high jump, placed parallel to each other and at least 10 feet apart. The judge tells the handler which jump the dog must go over, and the handler relays this message to the dog. After going over the correct jump, the dog returns to the handler and sits in front of him. The judge requests a finish, and then the entire procedure is repeated with the other jump.

The "honoring" exercise is required at all levels of UKC obedience competition. This means that a dog remains in the down position in a designated area of the ring while another dog is working through the exercises. In the honoring exercise, a dog is evaluated on how well he responds to his owner's down command, how he reacts (or does not react) to his handler's moving away from him and how he behaves while the other dog is working.

You may choose not to compete with your Goldendoodle in obedience trials, but he still will enjoy learning the obedience-trial exercises. Teaching these exercises will be challenging and fun for both of you. You don't need to spend money on equipment; for example, you can set up jumps by placing a board between two trees or two chairs. You can do the figure-8 around cones, bushes or the kids! You can teach the directed retrieve with your own gloves or other household items. Have fun!

Speaking of fun, let's talk about agility. Just going to an agility training class is a lot of fun. From there, you can decide if you'd like to progress to competition. There are plenty of opportunities for non-AKC breeds to compete and earn awards in agility trials.

With agility, the fun is in the learning. An agility course is essentially an obstacle course, and dogs learn to navigate each obstacle. As they become confident on the obstacles, the goal is to complete the course with speed and accuracy. Obstacles include A-frames, see-saws, different types of jumps, "dog-walks," tunnels, weave poles, crawl tubes and more. Agility is a real team effort, with both dog and owner participating, as you are with your dog on the course, issuing commands and encouragement to help him go through the exercises correctly. It's a fast-paced sport that your Goldendoodle will love, and it's also very popular with spectators.

Flyball is a relatively new sport, but one that has caught on quickly and is gaining in popularity. You should be able to find a training club in your area to get your Goldendoodle involved in this fun relay race. In a flyball race, there are normally four teams, each comprising four dogs and four handlers. They stand at one end and release the dogs, one at a time, to run down a lane (which has four jumps in advanced competition) and stomp on a board, which releases a tennis ball. The dog must catch the ball, run back to his handler and hand over the ball. Once the dog returns, the next dog is released. The first team to have all four dogs go through the course success-fully wins the race.

Another event that is becoming popular is rally obedience, called "Rally-O." This is a variation on obedience competition, with similar types of exercises, but Rally-O is timed. The heeling exercises in Rally-O are more difficult and varied than those in the obedience ring, involving spiraling and turning in different directions. It's much like a dance, but the exercises are numbered and must be completed in proper order as set forth by the judge. This is a challenging and quick activity, requiring dog and handler to think on their feet and keep moving—

sounds like it was made for the Goldendoodle!

We can't mention "dance" without mentioning freestyle, another great sport that is gaining devotees around the world. This is best described as "dancing with dogs." Freestyle events are open to all dogs, so this might be just the thing for you and your dancing Doodle. In freestyle competition, a single exhibitor and one or more dogs, or a team of exhibitors and dogs, perform a choreographed routine. For example, you might see an exhibitor walking backward while her dog weaves around her legs, or the pair performing turns in unison. For an imaginative choreographer and a well-trained dog, the routines can be quite elaborate. Usually the exhibitors wear some type of costume, with the dogs wearing something to match! The World Wide Freestyle Association is the leader in hosting and promoting freestyle events.

Like a Doodle to water...

KEEPING BUSY

Of course, organized activities aren't the only things you can do with your dog. As a Goldendoodle owner, you are blessed with an able-bodied, active and trainable dog who loves to be with you. You can enjoy so many things together—hiking, swimming, hunting and more. Golden-doodles love to run and swim, and don't forget that they come from sporting-dog heritage. Of course the Golden Retriever is known as one of the most popular sporting dogs, but the Poodle's history shows him as a prized hunting dog throughout Europe. Whatever you like to do, it will be more fun with a Goldendoodle!

Winston can't contain himself: "It's fun to be a Goldendoodle!"

Goldendoodles are never fair-weather friends.

This young lady and her Doodle "sibling" certainly see eye-to-eye.

It's a nice day for a seaside stroll with boy's best friend.

The joy of breeding Goldendoodles

Breeding the
Goldendoodle

As with any breeding program, the decision to embark on producing Goldendoodles is a serious one with many facets to be considered. It is best left to those with longtime experience in having litters, or previous experience with showing, the field and other related areas of animal husbandry and veterinary care. This is especially true for Goldendoodles, as they are continuing to evolve and develop as a designer dog, with wonderful discoveries of their capabilities always being made. Such discoveries emerge from careful planning by experienced breeders who choose the right members of the parent breeds for breeding stock or select the perfect Goldendoodle for future breeding. Within my own Make Way for Doodles breeding program, my Golden Retriever mothers have developed from my choosing the most lovable puppies with the best temperaments possible from litters coming from my very first Golden Retriever, and then so on down the line, so that the wonderful qualities I know so well continue to shine through in all of my offspring. I have done this similarly for my Golden Retriever studs that I use with my female Poodle for producing Goldendoodles, as temperament is every bit as important in male stud dogs. They were chosen as puppies from litters I raised specifically for the calm and outstanding temperaments that I personally admire in my pets. Because of the high quality of the Golden Retrievers, male and female alike, that I

is unmistakable on the face of a happy breeder.

use for breeding (including champion-line dogs from show Golden Retriever breeders), all of my Golden Retrievers also have the attributes of being very handsome and sound dogs in addition to possessing sweet, smart and very calm temperaments.

As author Beth J. Finder Harris cites in her book *Breeding a Litter*, geneticists believe that certain behaviors as well as the predisposition toward certain character traits "are about 10 percent inherited and the other 90 percent are acquired." This inherited 10 percent does, however, remain with the puppies as they grow into adults and throughout their lives. Therefore I consider it to be an important part of my responsibility as a breeder to stay very closely involved with my Goldendoodle puppies (and in the past with my Golden Retriever puppies), my parent dogs and before they are born and throughout their important weeks with me before they go to their loving new homes. I want to make sure that I know their temperaments well enough to ensure that I am still passing down the qualities that I have seen repeated for two decades and love so much in my own pets.

We will talk more about the importance of that early socialization, but first a little more discussion on choosing just the right parent stock and other things to which good breeders need to be attuned.

"They say I've got my father's ears."

STOCK CHOICES AND CROSSES

There are many reputable breeders in the Goldendoodle network whom I know and with whom I am associated. I would also like to add that breeders who are used to looking for temperament issues first, rather than conformational characteristics, also have no problem identifying fine pets to join their breeding programs. I am also very proud of my delightful Poodles, each unique in his/her own right, but every bit warm and wonderful enough to be family members with me and to pass on outstanding traits to their offspring.

To help you understand Goldendoodle terminology more clearly, I will use my own dogs as examples. My Standard Poodle, "Studley," so gracious and kingly he is, can be bred to any of my Golden Retriever mothers to produce what would be known as a "first-cross standard" Goldendoodle, which weighs between 46 and 90 pounds.

© KATHRYN YAMARINO

A colorful newborn litter of Doodles. The ribbon collars help the breeder monitor each pup's individual growth.

"Dandy Doodle," my smaller female Standard Poodle, could also be bred to my male Golden Retriever stud to produce first-cross Goldendoodle offspring, as it makes no difference if the mother is a Poodle and the father is a Golden Retriever, or the other way around. The puppies will still be Goldendoodles! It is important to note here that none of the parents of my Goldendoodles, of course, is related in any way, including my Poodles, to

The author's Poodle dam seems unfazed by her very demanding litter. What a sweet and willing mom!

avoid any of the complications that inbreeding can create.

Another promising and bright horizon in the world of breeding Goldendoodles is the arrival of the miniature Goldendoodle. I also have a chocolate Miniature Poodle stud who could be bred (via artificial insemination) with any of my female Golden Retrievers to produce what is known as a "first-cross miniature" Goldendoodle (weighing 17–45 pounds).

These first-cross standard or miniature Goldendoodles are the best examples of the phenomenon of hybrid vigor—one of the most alluring traits of Goldendoodles—for this type of cross produces the best pairing of genetic material from two pure-bred dog gene pools that are completely unrelated. I add to that by noting again that the miniatures are being produced via artificial insemination, and thus far, by all reports and feedback, are resulting in fabulous Goldendoodles that are excelling in all areas and surpassing the standards in some areas. For example, the PADS training program in California, which prepares dogs to work as assistance dogs for the hearing-impaired, has had limited success with standard Goldendoodles but, thus far, great success with the miniatures in readying them to serve as hearing dogs.

Now that we have learned about the first-cross Doodles, let's talk about the F_{1B} or "first-cross backcross" litter, which means breeding a Goldendoodle with a Miniature Poodle to produce miniature F_{1B} Goldendoodles or with a Standard Poodle to produce standard F_{1B} Goldendoodles.

The principle reason that breeders would breed the F_{1B} litter would be to increase the hypoallergenic nature of the dogs. This is a frequent request from owners who have children who suffer from severe allergies. A Goldendoodle "backcross" to a Poodle should result in even better hypoallergenic qualities than that of the F_1 Goldendoodle, while still maintaining the great Golden Retriever temperament and loyalty as a family pet. The backcross

Goldendoodle offspring would have 25 percent more Poodle genes than an F_1 Goldendoodle, with the presumption of even greater hypoallergenic properties (with a hybrid, it remains a presumption, never a 100-percent guarantee).

Golden Retrievers make splendid, loving moms, too.

Another fun aspect of backcrossing is the prospect of a whole rainbow of Goldendoodle colors, as the introduction of more Poodle genes enables a myriad of new color possibilities for our Goldendoodles of the future. Remember, Golden Retrievers only come in one color: golden (though the shades vary greatly); Poodles come in dozens of colors and even parti-colors (which are frowned upon by pure-bred fanciers). While the prospect of producing miniature "chocodoodles" and standard "parti-doodles" may be amusing (and delicious), the exciting truth is that the puppies in such a litter could be seen in many different colors, including cream with black or light brown noses, parti-colored (brown and white or black and white), solid black, solid brown in a range of shades, silvery, redder shades and the light coloration traditionally seen in Goldendoodles.

There are now several organizations that can test for Poodle dominant and recessive color genes, or alleles. We won't get too technical for the purposes of this book, but breeders can determine, via testing or by the offspring that they produce, the dominant and recessive color genes that their Poodles or Goldendoodles carry. They then will be able to match up future sires and dams to try to produce certain colors in the Doodle offspring.

A few more words here about backcrossing with regard to hypoallergenic properties, shedding concerns and Goldendoodle coats. One thing that I have found in breeding Goldendoodles is that my first-cross dogs have produced very few allergic responses in people who had allergies. Either the owners are not having any adverse reactions or the owners love their Doodles enough to tolerate any slight allergic responses and are not reporting any allergic reactions back to me.

Shedding is slightly different. Some Goldendoodles shed a little; some not at all. There is some shedding when Doodles lose their puppy coats before the adult coats come in, but it is not at all like the shedding you would see with a Golden Retriever and, for the most part, it passes quickly. It is, therefore, very minimal.

Wonderfully intriguing about Goldendoodle litters is the vast difference between their puppy-coat appearances and their adult coats, especially when you compare this to the coat of a Golden Retriever. Golden Retriever puppies' coats tend to darken as they get older, while Goldendoodle puppies' coats tend to lighten more often than not. An apricot puppy can surprise you by becoming a fluffy white Doodle adult, perhaps with slight golden-tipped ends on his curly coat. A light-colored puppy can become a more golden-colored adult.

In certain rare instances, a Goldendoodle breeder might choose to backcross his Goldendoodle bitch to a Golden Retriever stud. A breeder may opt to use a Goldendoodle bitch who has an excellent temperament and/or a beautiful coat to backcross to a Golden Retriever stud in order to further enhance a Golden Retriever quality that he would like to see more of in the offspring. This only occurs if the breeder feels that he will not be compromising any of the qualities already achieved in the previous crossing. Such a mating, or backcrossing, requires great breeder skill and knowledge of one's dogs and should not be undertaken lightly, as the majority of backcrossings are to Poodles generally for improving hypoallergenic qualities.

Careless ignorance in backcrossing or breeding generally is precisely how previous hybrids have become diluted and their future potential clouded, if not ruined forever. In this way, their intelligence and temperaments, so full of potential in the beginning, have been ruined by ignorant opportunists. These same words apply to those who may be seeking to breed Golden-doodle to Goldendoodle. Every mating of a Golden-doodle to a Goldendoodle may vastly dilute any benefits of hybrid vigor, unless done by extremely qualified breeders who are thoroughly versed in their bloodlines and have specific goals for the breeding.

The Goldendoodle
standard would say:
"perfection measured in
joy and joy alone."

HEALTH SCREENING

The reader is thus cautioned: all Goldendoodles are *not* the same. You serve the future of the Goldendoodle well to seek out only the most sincere, experienced and reputable Goldendoodle breeders with quality parent stock who are producing first-cross (or possibly F_{1B}) Goldendoodles. Remember to seek out those breeders with seals of approval as recommended Golden-doodles.com breeders.

Each Goldendoodle is unique unto itself, and I marvel and rejoice in the fact that there is no "breed standard" for Goldendoodles, no printed guidelines to describe the ideal outward appearance of the "perfect Goldendoodle." In the author's opinion, the "perfect Goldendoodle" is any healthy, long-lived, loving dog who gives joy to his owner and family. While many diseases continue to plague our beautiful pure-bred parent breeds, there always remain idiopathic health concerns for all, human and canine. Provided a breeder is using the best possible pure-bred Golden Retriever and Poodle parent stock, the author truly believes that hybrid vigor in theory and practice, if applied well, is the best starting point for a healthier family pet.

Along with the temperament that I value highly, of course, is the health of the parents. All quality breeders test their breeding stock regularly for hip dysplasia via preliminary and permanent Orthopedic Foundation for Animals (OFA) or PennHIP radiograph methods of testing. They also have yearly tests done for eye issues with the Canine Eye Registration Foundation (CERF), which issues certification to eligible breeding dogs and cites minor eye issues that breeders can keep track of in determining suitable breeding match-ups. For example, if an intended mother-to-be has a benign eyelash condition noted on an exam, the breeder may decide to use a stud that does not have the same eyelash condition noted on his CERF exam. In this way, the breeder does not double up on the condition lest it manifest itself in the offspring as something more serious.

Some breeders also may prefer to do further testing on

Dr. Aubin performing a CERF exam. Puppies that come from two CERF-cleared parents are at an advantage to inheriting healthy eyes themselves.

recurring genetic maladies.

A further issue is the problem of prejudice against Goldendoodle breeders by pure-bred breeders, which can make it hard for Doodle breeders to attain quality breeding stock from proven breeders. This is most unfair in many respects, but also was extant prior to the onset of hybrids. Good breeders are often very reluctant to share their breeding stock with unknown breeders. Unfortunately this occurs because of a few very bad owners who have lied to hard-working quality breeders, obtained puppies from them under false pretenses and bred them indiscriminately or without permission, or without the compensation due the breeders via breeding agreements. To breed Goldendoodles whose parents have not been health-tested, or by using inappropriate studs or improper backcrossing methods, is highly irresponsible. Potential puppy buyers again are cautioned away from such opportunists and are urged to research and ask proper questions of Doodle breeders they are considering.

their breeding stock for rarer diseases if they have cause to suspect them in their breeding stock. There often is great difficulty for quality breeders internationally to find and retain good breeding stock, as a breeder can raise Golden Retrievers or Poodles diligently as part of their programs only to find later on that they have hip or eye problems that discount them from producing offspring. The pure-bred lines are, quite frankly, fraught with

RESPONSIBILITIES AND COMMITMENT

In our discussion of breeding Goldendoodles, I am purposely omitting any discussion of actual breeding techniques, as any novice who is interested in breeding should not be learning how to do so from a book. The assistance of an experienced breeder or a veterinarian is needed for those who are seeking to embark on their own breeding programs. Many things can go wrong, resulting in injury to the breeding animals or causing an otherwise suitable breeding dog to have an aversion to being bred.

Also, anyone wishing to become a breeder must know that there are inordinate financial costs involved in breeding, as well as emotional and moral responsibilities. You become the parent and guiding light to the living things that you bring into the world. You owe them first and foremost the best possible quality of life. If you are not able to make such a commitment of the money, time and hard work required for breeding dogs, then you should not be breeding animals. Consider the case of a sickly pup in need of advanced medical care; you must be prepared and have the resources to provide that pup and every pup with the minute-to-minute care that they need to thrive and grow.

At two days old, the pups are all in agreement: "Feed us!"

A hungry young litter, gathering 'round at chow time!

Doodle litter, on the march.

PREGNANCY, WHELPING AND REARING

So now our female is pregnant and expecting! Plenty of fresh air, sunshine, exercise, play, normal routine, love, interaction, healthy diet, up-to-date on all shots and free of ticks, fleas and other parasites—these things are all given! Some veterinarians and authorities on breeding and whelping recommend vitamin and mineral supplementation of the mother's diet during pregnancy and whelping, and others recommend just maintaining steady nutrition with an increased normal diet and offering many smaller meals throughout the day as the mother's girth increases and birth nears. What is universally agreed upon is that overdoing the dam's vitamin and mineral supplementation can be detrimental to the bitch and puppies. So caution is advised, and every good breeder has his own special ways of maintaining maternal and fetal health, usually in close association with his veterinarian. A high-quality balanced dog food, increased to one-and-a-half times the

There's no doubt that this pup has inherited cuteness.

dog's normal intake in the last weeks before birth, is usually fine and foregoes any nutritional imbalances that supplementations may cause.

Birth or whelping usually occurs about 57 days after mating. A nice, quiet, out-of-the-way place for the mother is ideal. A specially made whelping box with rails around the sides to prevent the mother from lying on her puppies, and to permit the puppies to move freely out from under her, can prevent sad losses of puppies from inadvertent suffocation. I, and

other breeders whom I know, often spend the first week or two sleeping next to a mother and newborn puppies in order to listen for any sounds of distress and make sure that a tired mother has not accidentally repositioned herself on top of a puppy. This is among the top causes of losing puppies within a litter early on.

Placing the whelping box in an area where the puppies will be kept warm and free from any drafts is also important, as cold puppies do not nurse and they may become hypoglycemic, go into seizures and die. Puppies cannot regulate their own body temperatures for the first several weeks.

Delivering a litter often can take many hours. It is important for the mother to have a loving breeder close by to assist her in making sure that each newborn pup finds a teat for his share of mother's milk. Colostrum, the important ingredient found in the mother's milk, passes many immunities on to the puppies to protect them until they begin building their own immunities with vaccinations. The breeder can also assist a tired mother in tearing the pups' fetal sacs. This clears the way for the awesome thrill of the very first breath of Goldendoodle life, which always exhilarates and gives such wonderful and inspiring joy.

Having an attentive and caring breeder close by to comfort the mother, pat her and speak calmly to her also has great merit for the puppies. I firmly believe, again as Beth J. Finder Harris does in *Breeding a Litter*, that the "neonatal period," from birth

to eight to ten weeks of life, is of utmost import to a Goldendoodle puppy. It is at this time that the pups acquire much of their mother's temperament "as the result of their intense focus and relationship with their mother." If the mother is "confident of her role and position within the household and she is openly and outwardly friendly, these character traits will be acquired by her progeny. Puppies and older dogs can and do learn from each other and those closest to them."

On the contrary, puppies that are born to a nervous, weak mother into a tumultuous, cold, unstimulating environment where all must struggle daily for survival, or seldom have human companionship, can have many negatives communicated to them by their mother and their environment with lifelong ramifications.

Remember that inherited predisposition toward certain behaviors is thought to be about 10 percent inherited and 90 percent acquired. Harris goes on to note that the "environment in which a litter is raised, therefore, is of paramount importance to having well-socialized and confident puppies." As a breeder, I have found this to be absolutely true.

My "Doodlets" immediately become very much welcomed and loved members of the household and family during their time with me, and are positively "home-raised." Their training for new homes and their lifelong character traits thus begin here with me as they take their very first breaths. This is how it should be with all quality breeders and how it is with many. I am proud to know many such breeders in the Goldendoodle network of which I am a part.

Inquiries about my puppies and inquiries to other quality breeders about their puppies often come to us via the Internet at www.Golden-doodles.com or through our individual websites. I am a recommended Golden-doodles.com breeder, and my website is www.makewayfor-doodles.com. Remember that Goldendoodles.com is the best way to begin searching for a quality Goldendoodle. You will find many fine like-minded breeders and much additional information on this awesome designer dog.

You've come to the tail end...is this the Doodle dog for you?

INDEX